The Atharvaveda

The Atharvaveda

Translated from the Sanskrit by

Maurice Bloomfield

First published 1897

DID YOU KNOW...?

You can read any and all of our _thousands_ *of books online for*

FREE

Just visit:

www.forgottenbooks.org

PUBLISHER'S PREFACE

About the Book

"The Atharvaveda (atharvaveda, a tatpurusha compound of atharvan, a type of priest, and veda meaning "knowledge") is a sacred text of Hinduism, and one of the four Vedas, often called the "fourth Veda". According to tradition, the Atharvaveda was mainly composed by two groups of rishis known as the Bhrigus and the Angirasas. Additionally, tradition ascribes parts to other rishis, such as Kausika, Vasistha and Kashyapa. There are two surviving recensions (sakhas), known as Saunakiya (AVS) and Paippalada (AVP).

The Atharvaveda, while undoubtedly belonging to the core Vedic corpus, in some ways represents an independent parallel tradition to that of the Rigveda and Yajurveda."

(Quote from wikipedia.org)

CONTENTS

PUBLISHER'S PREFACE VII

EXCERPT FROM THE INTRODUCTION.. 1

CHARMS TO CURE DISEASES AND POSSESSION BY DEMONS OF DISEASE
(BHAISHAGYKNI) 3

PRAYERS FOR LONG LIFE AND HEALTH (ÂYUSHYÂNI)................................ 42

IMPRECATIONS AGAINST DEMONS, SORCERERS, AND ENEMIES
(ÂBHIKÂRIKÂNI AND KRITYÂPRATIHARANÂNI)............................... 54

CHARMS PERTAINING TO WOMEN (STRIKARATÂNI)................................... 79

CHARMS PERTAINING TO ROYALTY (RÂGAKARMÂNI).............................. 93

CHARMS TO SECURE HARMONY, INFLUENCE IN THE ASSEMBLY, AND THE
LIKE (SÂMMANASYÂNI, ETC.)... 111

CHARMS TO SECURE PROSPERITY IN HOUSE, FIELD, CATTLE, BUSINESS,
GAMBLING, AND KINDRED MATTERS 116

CHARMS IN EXPIATION OF SIN AND DEFILEMENT................................... 135

PRAYERS AND IMPRECATIONS IN THE INTEREST OF THE BRAHMANS 140

COSMOGONIC AND THEOSOPHIC HYMNS.. 164

EXCERPT FROM THE INTRODUCTION

THE present volume of translations comprises about one third of the entire material of the Atharva-veda in the text of the Saunaka-school. But it represents the contents and spirit of the fourth Veda in a far greater measure than is indicated by this numerical statement. The twentieth book of the Samhitâ, with the exception of the so-called kuntâpasûktini (hymns 127-136), seems to be a verbatim repetition of mantras contained in the Rig-veda, being employed in the Vaitâna-sûra at the sastras and stotras of the soma-sacrifice: it is altogether foreign to the spirit of the original Atharvan. The nineteenth book is a late addendum, in general very corrupt; its omission (with the exception of hymns 26, 34, 35, 38, 39, 53, and 54) does not detract much from the general impression left by the body of the collection. The seventeenth book consists of a single hymn of inferior interest. Again, books XV and XVI, the former entirely Brahmanical prose, the latter almost entirely so, are of doubtful quality and chronology. Finally, books XIV and XVIII contain respectively the wedding and funeral stanzas of the Atharvan, and are largely coincident with corresponding Mantras of the tenth book of the Rig-veda: they are, granted their intrinsic interest, not specifically Atharvanic. Of the rest of the Atharvan (books I-XIII) there is presented here about one half, naturally that half which seemed to the translator the most interesting and characteristic. Since not a little of the collection rises scarcely above the level of mere verbiage, the process of exclusion has not called for any great degree of abstemiousness.

These successive acts of exclusion have made it possible to present a fairly complete history of each of the hymns translated. The employment of the hymns in the Atharvanic practices is in closer touch with the original purpose of the composition or compilation of the hymns than is true in the case of the other collections of Vedic hymns. Many times, though by no means at all times, the practices connected with a given hymn present the key to the correct interpretation of the hymn itself. In any case it is instructive to see what the Atharvan priests did with the hymns of their own school, even if we must judge their performances to be secondary.

I do not consider any translation of the AV. at this time as final. The most difficult problem, hardly as yet ripe for final solution, is the original function of many mantras, after they have been stripped of certain adaptive modifications, imparted to them to meet the immediate purpose of the Atharvavedin. Not infrequently a stanza has to be rendered in some measure of harmony with its connection, when, in fact, a more original meaning, not at all applicable to its present environment, is but scantily covered up by the secondary modifications of the text. This garbled tradition of the ancient texts partakes of the character of popular etymology in the course of the transmission of wofds. New meaning is read into the mantras, and any little stubbornness on their part is met with modifications of their wording. The critic encounters here a very difficult situation: searching investigation of the remaining Vedic collections is necessary before a bridge can be built from the more original meaning to the meaning implied and required by the situation in a given Atharvan hymn. Needless to say the only correct and useful way to translate a mantra in the Atharvan, is to reproduce it with the bent which it has received in the Atharvan. The other Vedic collections are by no means free from the same taint. The entire Vedic tradition, the Rig-veda not excepted, presents rather the conclusion than the beginning of a long period of literary activity. Conventionality of subject-matter, style, form (metre), &c., betray themselves at every step: the 'earliest' books of the RV. are not exempt from the same processes of secondary grouping and adaptation of their mantras, though these are less frequent and less obvious than is the case in the Atharva-veda.

Obligations to previous translators: Weber, Muir, Ludwig, Zimmer, Grill', Henry, &c., are acknowledged in the introduction to each hymn. I regret that the work was in the hands of the printer prior to the appearance of Professor Henry's excellent version of books X-XII. The late lamented Professor Whitney kindly furnished me with the advance sheets of the late Shankar Pandurang Pandit's scholarly edition of the AV. with Sâyana's commentary, as also with many of the readings of the Cashmir text (the so-called Paippalâda-sâkhâ) of the AV. Neither the Paippalâda nor Sâyana sensibly relieves the task of its difficulty and responsibility.

MAURICE BLOOMFIELD.

BALTIMORE: April, 1896.

CHARMS TO CURE DISEASES AND POSSESSION BY DEMONS OF DISEASE (BHAISHAGYKNI)

V, 22. Charm against takman (fever) and related diseases

1. May Agni drive the takman away from here, may Soma, the press-stone, and Varuna, of tried skill; may the altar, the straw (upon the altar), and the brightly-flaming fagots (drive him away)! Away to naught shall go the hateful powers!

2. Thou that makest all men sallow, inflaming them like a searing fire, even now, O takman, thou shalt become void of strength: do thou now go away down, aye, into the depths!

The takman that is spotted, covered Nvith spots, like reddish sediment, him thou, (O plant) of unremitting potency, drive away down below!

4. Having made obeisance to the takman, I cast him down below: let him, the champion of Sakambhara, return again to the Mahâvrishas!

5. His home is with the Mûgavants, his home with the Mahâvrishas. From the moment of thy birth thou art indigenous with the Balhikas.

6. O takman, vyâla, vîgada, vyânga, hold off (thy missile) far! Seek the gadabout slave-girl, strike her with thy bolt!

7. O takman, go to the Mûgavants, or to the Balhikas farther away! Seek the lecherous Sûdra female: her, O takman, give a good shaking-up!

8. Go away to the Mahâvrishas and the Mûgavants, thy kinsfolk, and consume them! Those (regions) do we bespeak for the takman, or these regions here other (than ours).

9. (If) in other regions thou dost not abide, mayest thou that art powerful take pity on us! Takman, now, has become eager: he will go to the Balhikas.

10. When thou, being cold, and then again deliriously hot, accompanied by cough, didst cause the (sufferer) to shake, then, O takman, thy missiles were terrible: from these surely exempt us!

11. By no means ally thyself with balâsa, cough and spasm! From there do thou not return hither again: that, O takman, do I ask of thee!

12. O takman, along with thy brother balâsa, along with thy sister cough, along with thy cousin pâman, go to yonder foreign folk!

13. Destroy the takman that returns on (each) third day, the one that intermits (each) third day, the one that continues without intermission, and the autumnal one; destroy the cold takman, the hot, him that comes in summer, and him that arrives in the rainy season!

14. To the Gandhâris, the Mâgavants, the Angas, and the Magadhas, we deliver over the takman, like a servant, like a treasure!

VI, 20. Charm against takman (fever)

1. As if from this Agni (fire), that burns and flashes, (the takman) comes. Let him then, too, as a babbling drunkard, pass away! Let him, the impious one, search out some other person, not ourselves! Reverence be to the takman with the burning weapon!

2. Reverence be to Rudra, reverence to the takman, reverence to the luminous king Varuna! Reverence to heaven, reverence to earth, reverence to the plants!

3. To thee here, that burnest through, and turnest all bodies yellow, to the red, to the brown, to the takman produced by the forest, do I render obeisance.

I, 25. Charm against takman (fever)

1. When Agni, having entered the waters, burned, where the (gods) who uphold the order (of the universe) rendered homage (to Agni), there, they say, is thy origin on high: do thou feel for us, and spare us, O takman!

2. Whether thou art flame, whether thou art heat, or whether from licking chips (of wood) thou bast arisen, Hrûdu by name art thou, O god of the yellow: do thou feel for us, and spare us, O takman!

3. Whether thou art burning, whether thou art scorching, or whether thou art the son of king Varuna, Hrûdu by name art thou, O god of the yellow: do thou feel for us, and spare us, O takman!

4. To the cold takman, and to the deliriously hot, the glowing, do I render homage. To hirn that returns on the morrow, to him that returns for two (successive) days, to the takman that returns on the third day, homage shall be!

VII, 116. Charm against takman (fever)

1. Homage (be) to the deliriously hot, the shaking, exciting, impetuous (takman)! Homage to the cold (takman), to him that in the past fulfilled desires!

2. May (the takman) that returns on the morrow, he that returns on two (successive) days, the impious one, pass into this frog!

V, 4. Prayer to the kushtha-plant to destroy takman (fever)

1. Thou that art born upon the mountains, as the most potent of plants, come hither, O kushtha, destroyer of the takman, to drive out from here the takman!

2. To thee (that growest) upon the mountain, the brooding-place of the eagle, (and) art sprung from Himavant, they come with treasures, having heard (thy fame). For they know (thee to be) the destroyer of the takman.

3. The asvattha-tree is the seat of the gods in the third heaven from here. There the gods procured the kushtha, the visible manifestation of amrita (ambrosia).

4. A golden ship with golden tackle moved upon the heavens. There the gods procured the kushtha, the flower of amrita (ambrosia).

5. The paths were golden, and golden were the oars; golden were the ships, upon which they carried forth the kushtha hither (to the mountain).

6. This person here, O kushtha, restore for me, and cure him! Render him free from sickness for me!

7. Thou art born of the gods, thou art Soma's good friend. Be thou propitious to my in-breathing and my out-breathing, and to this eye of mine!

8. Sprung in the north from the Himavant (mountains), thou art brought to the people in the east. There the most stiperior varieties of the kushtha were apportioned.

9. 'Superior,' O kushtha, is thy name; 'superior' is the name of thy father. Do thou drive out all disease, and render the takman devoid of strength!

10. Pain in the head, affliction in the eye, and ailment of the body, all that shall the kushtha heal-a divinely powerful (remedy), forsooth!

XIX, 39. Prayer to the kushtha-plant to destroy takman (fever), and other ailments

1. May the protecting god kushtha come hither from the Himavant: destroy thou every takman, and all female spooks!

2. Three names hast thou, O kushtha, (namely: kushtha), na-ghâ-mâra ('forsooth-no-death'), and na-ghâ-risha ('forsooth-no-harm'). Verily no harm shall suffer (na ghâ . . . rishat) this person here, for whom I bespeak thee morn and eve, aye the (entire) day!

3. Thy mother's name is gîvalâ ('quickening'), thy father's name is gîvanta ('living'). Verily no harm shall suffer this person here, for whom I bespeak thee morn and eve, aye the entire day!

4. Thou art the most superior of the plants, as a steer among cattle, as the tiger among beasts of prey. Verily no harm shall stiffer this person here, for whom I bespeak thee morn and eve, aye the entire day!

5. Thrice begotten by the Sâmbu Angiras, thrice by the Âdityas, and thrice by all the gods, this kushtha, a universal remedy, stands together with soma. Destroy thou every takman, and all female spooks!

6. The asvattha-tree is the seat of the gods in the third heaven from here. There came to sight the amrita (ambrosia), there the kushtha-plant was born.

7. A golden ship with golden tackle moved upon the heavens. There came to sight the amrita, there the kushtha-plant was born.

8. On the spot where the ship glided down, on the peak of the Himavant, there came to sight the ambrosia, there the kushtha-plant was born. This kushtha, a universal remedy, stands together with soma. Destroy thou every takman, and all female spooks!

9. (We know) thee whom Ikshvâku knew of yore, whom the women, fond of kushtha, knew, whom Vâyasa and Mâtsya knew: therefore art thou a universal remedy.

10. The takman that returns on each third day, the one that cominues without intermission, and the yearly one, ao thou, (O plant) of unremitting strength, drive away down below!

I, 12. Prayer to lightning, conceived as the cause of fever, headache, and cough

1. The first red bull, born of the (cloud-)womb, born of wind and clouds, comes on thundering with rain. May he, that cleaving moves straight on, spare our bodies; he who, a single force, has passed through threefold!

2. Bowing down to thee that fastenest thyself with heat upon every limb, we would reverence thee with oblations; we would reverence with oblations the crooks and hooks of thee that hast, as a seizer, seized the limbs of this person.

3. Free him from headache and also from cough, (produced by the lightning) that has entered his every joint! May the flashing (lightning), that is born of the cloud, and born of the wind, strike the trees and the mountains!

4. Comfort be to my upper limb, comfort be to my nether; comfort be to my four members, comfort to my entire body!

I, 22. Charm against jaundice and related diseases

1. Up to the sun shall go thy heart-ache and thy jaundice: in the colour of the red bull do we eovelop thee!

2. We envelop thee in red tints, unto long life. May this person go unscathed, and be free of yellow colour!

3. The cows whose divinity is Rohini, they who, moreover, axe (themselves) red (róhinin)-(in their) every form and every strength we do envelop thee.

4. Into the parrots, into the ropanâkâs (thrush) do we put thy jaundice, and, furthermore, into the hâridravas (yellow wagtail) do we put thy jaundice.

VI, 14. Charm against the disease balâsa

1. The internal disease that has set in, that crumbles the bones, and crumbles the joints, every balâsa do thou drive out, that which is in the limbs, and in the joints!

2. The balâsa of him that is afflicted with balâsa do I remove, as one gelds a lusty animal. Its connection do I cut off as the root of a pumpkin.

3. Fly forth from here, O balâsa, as a swift foal (after the mare). And even, as the reed in every year, pass away without slaying men!

VI, 105. Charm against cough

1. As the-soul with the soul's desires swiftly to a distance flies, thus do thou, O cough, fly forth along the soul's course of flight!

2. As a well-sharpened arrow swiftly to a distance flies, thus do thou, O cough, fly forth along the expanse of the earth!

3. As the rays of the sun swiftly to a distance fly, thus do thou, O cough, fly forth along the flood of the sea!

I, 2. Charm against excessive discharges from the body

1. We know the father of the arrow, Parg-anya, who furnishes bountiful fluid, and well do we know his mother, Prithivi (earth), the multiform!

2. O bowstring, turn aside from us, turn my body into stone! Do thou firmly hold very far away the hostile powers and the haters!

3. When the bowstring, embracing the wood (of the bow), greets with a whiz the eaoer arrow, do thou, O Indra, ward off from us the piercing missile!

4. As the point (of the arrow) stands in the way of heaven and earth, thus may the muñga-grass unfailingly stand in the way of sickness and (excessive) discharge!

II, 3. Charm against excessive discharges from the body, undertaken with spring-water

1. The spring-water yonder which runs down upon the mountain, that do I render healing for thee, in order that thou mayest contain a potent remedy.

2. Then surely, yea quite surely, of the hundred remedies contained in thee, thou art the most superior in checking discharges and removing pain.

3. Deep down do the Asuras bury this great healer of wounds: that is the cure for discharges, and thal hath removed disease.

4. The ants bring the remedy from the sea: that is the cure for discharges, and that hath quieted disease.
5. This great healer of wounds has been gotten out of the earth: that is the cure for discharges, and
that hath removed disease.
6. May the waters afford us welfare, may the herbs be propitious to us I Indra's bolt shall beat off the Rakshas, far (from us) shall fly the arrows cast by the Rakshas!

VI, 44. Charm against excessive discharges from the body

1. The heavens have stood still, the earth has stood still, all creatures have stood still. The trees that sleep erect have stood still: may this disease of thine stand still!

2. Of the hundred remedies which thou hast, of the thousand that have been collected, this is the most excellent cure for discharges, the best remover of disease.

3. Thou art the urine of Rudra, the navel of amrita (ambrosia). Thy name, forsooth, is vishânakâ, (thou art) arisen from the foundation of the Fathers, a remover of diseases produced by the winds (of the body).

I, 3. Charm against constipation and retention of urine

1. We know the father of the arrow, Parganya, of hundredfold power. With this (charm) may I render comfortable thy body: make thy Outpouring upon the earth; out of thee may it come with the sound bâl!

2. We know the father of the arrow, Mitra, &c.
3. We know the father of the arrow, Varuna, &c.
4. We know the father of the arrow, Kandra, &c.
5. We know the father of the arrow, Sûrya, &c.
6. That which has accumulated in thy entralls. thy canals, in thy bladder- thus let thy urine be released, out completely, with the sound bâl!

7, I split open thy penis like the dike of a lake--thus let thy urine be released, out completely, with the sound bâl!

8. Relaxed is the opening of thy bladder like the ocean, the reservoir of water--thus let thy urine be released, out completely, with the sound bâl!

9. As an arrow flies to a distance when hurled from the bow-thus let thy urine be released, out completely, with the sound bâl!

VI, 90. Charm against internal pain (colic), due to the missiles of Rudra

1. The arrow that Rudra did cast upon thee, into (thy) limbs, and into thy heart, this here do we now draw out away from thee.

2. From the hundred arteries which are distributed along thy limbs, from all of these do we exorcise forth the poisons.

3. Adoration be to thee, O Rudra, as thou casteth (thy arrow); adoration to the (arrow) when it has been placed upon (the bow); adoration to it as it is being hurled; adoration to it when it has fallen down!

I, 10. Charm against dropsy

1. This Asura rules over the gods; the commands of Varuna, the ruler, surely come true. From this (trouble), from the wrath of the mighty (Varuna), do I, excelling in my incantation, lead out this man.

2. Reverence, O king Varuna, be to thy wrath, for all falsehood, O mighty one, clost thou discover. A thousand others together do I make over to thee: this thy (man) shall live a hundred autumns!

3. From the untruth which thou hast spoken, the abundant wrong, with thy tongue--from king, Varuna I release thee, whose laws do not fail.

4. I release thee from Vaisvânara (Agni), from the great flood. Our rivals, O mighty one, do thou censure here, and give heed to our prayer!

VII, 83. Charm against dropsy

1. Thy golden chamber, king Varuna, is built in the waters! Thence the king that maintains the laws shall loosen all shackles!

2. From every habitation (of thine), O king Varuna, from here do thou free us! In that we have said, 'ye waters, ye cows;' in that we have said, 'O Varuna,' from this (sin), O Varuna, free us!

3. Lift from us, O Varuna, the uppermost fetter, take down the nethermost, loosen the middlemost! Then shall we, O Âditya, in thy law, exempt from guilt, live in freedom!

4. Loosen from us, O Varuna, all fetters, the uppermost, the nethermost, and those imposed by Varuna! Evil dreams, and misfortune drive away from us: then may we go to the world of the pious!

VI, 24. Dropsy, heart-disease, and kindred maladies cured by flowing water

1. From the Himavant (mountains) they flow forth, in the Sindhu (Indus), forsooth, is their assembling-place: may the waters, indeed, grant me that cure for heart-ache!

2. The pain that hurts me in the eyes, and that which hurts in the heels and the fore-feet, the waters, the most skilled of physicians, shall put all that to rights!

3. Ye rivers all, whose mistress is Sindhu, whose queen is Sindhu, grant us the remedy for that: through this (remedy) may we derive benefit from you!

VI, 80. An oblation to the sun, conceived as one of the two heavenly dogs, as a cure for paralysis

1. Through the air he flies, looking down upon all beings: with the majesty of the heavenly dog, with that oblation would we pay homage to thee!

2. The three kâlakâñga that are fixed upon the sky like gods, all these I have called for help, to render this person exempt from injury.

3. In the waters is thy origin, upon the heavens thy home, in the middle of the sea, and upon the earth thy greatness. With the majesty of the heavenly dog, with that oblation would we pay homage to thee!

II, 8. Charm against kshetriya, hereditary disease

1. Up have risen the majestic twin stars, the vikritau ('the two looseners'); may they loosen the nethermost and the uppermost fetter of the kshetriya (inherited disease)!

2. May this night shine (the kshetriya) away, may she shine away the witches; may the plant, destructive of kshetriya, shine the kshetriya away!

3. With the straw of thy brown barley, endowed with white stalks, with the blossom of the sesame--may the plant, destructive of kshetriya, shine the: kshetriya away!

4. Reverence be to thy ploughs, reverence to thy wagon-poles and yokes! May the plant, destructive of kshetriya, shine the kshetriya away!

5. Reverence be to those with sunken eyes reverence to the indicenous (evils?), reverence to the lord of the field! May the plant, destructive of kshetriya, shine the kshetriya away!

II, 10. Charm against kshetriya, hereditary disease

1. From kshetriya (inherited disease), from Nirriti (the goddess of destruction), from the curse of the kinswoman, from Druh (the demon of guile), from the fetter of Varuna do I release thee. Guiltless do I render thee through my charm; may heaven and earth both be propitious to thee!

2. May Agni together with the waters be auspicious to thee, may Soma together with the plants be auspicious. Thus from kshetriya, from Nirriti, from the curse of the kinswoman, from the Druh, from the fetter of Varuna do I release thee. Guiltless do I render thee through my charm; may heaven and earth both be propitious to thee!

May the wind in the atmosphere auspiciously bestow upon thee strength, may the four quarters of the heaven be auspicious to thee. Thus from kshetriya, from Nirriti &c.

4. These four goddesses, the directions of space, the consorts of the wind, the sun surveys. Thus from kshetriya, from Nirriti &c.

5. Within these (directions) I assign thee to old age; forth to a distance shall go Nirriti and disease! Thus from kshetriya, from Nirriti &c.

6. Thou hast been released from disease, from mishap, and from blame; out from the fetter of Druh, and from Grâhi (the demon of fits) thou hast been released. Thus from kshetriya, from Nirriti &c.

7. Thou didst leave behind Arâti (the demon of grudge), didst obtain prosperity, didst enter the happy world of the pious. Thus from kshetriya, from Nirriti &c.

8. The gods, releasing the sun and the ritam (the divine order of the universe) from darkness and from Grâhi, did take them out of sin. Thus from kshetriya, from Nirriti &c.

III, 7. Charm against kshetriya, hereditary disease

1. Upon the head of the nimble antelope a remedy grows! He has driven the kshetriya (inherited disease) in all directions by means of the horn.

2. The antelope has gone after thee with his four feet. O horn, loosen the kshetriya that is knitted into his heart!

3. (The horn) that glistens yonder like a roof with four wings (sides), with that do we drive out every kshetriya from thy limbs.

4. The lovely twin stars, the vikritau ('the two looseners') that are yonder upon the sky, shall loosen the nethermost and the uppermost fetter of the kshetriya!

5. The waters, verily, are healers, the waters are scatterers of disease, the waters cure all disease: may they. relieve thee from the kshetriya!

6. The kshetriya that has entered into thee from the prepared (magic) concoction, for that I know the remedy; I drive the kshetriya out of thee.

7. When the constellations fade away, and when the dawn does fade away, (then) shall he shine away from us every evil and the kshetriya!

I, 23. Leprosy cured by a dark plant

1. Born by night art thou, O plant, dark, black, sable. Do thou, that art rich in colour, stain this leprosy, and the gray spots!

2. The leprosy and the gray spots drive away from here--may thy native colour settle upon thee--the white spots cause to fly away!

3. Sable is thy hiding-place, sable thy dwelling-place, sable art thou, O plant: drive away from here the speckled spots!

4. The leprosy which has originated in the bones, and that which has originated in the body and upon the skin, the white mark begotten of corruption, I have destroyed with my charm.

I, 24. Leprosy cured by a dark plant

1. The eagle (suparna) that was born at first, his gall thou wast, O plant. The Âsurî having conquered this (gall) gave it to the trees for their colour.

2. The Âsurî was the first to construct this remedy for leprosy, this destroyer of leprosy. She has destroyed the leprosy, has made the skin of even colour.

3. 'Even-colour' is the name of thy mother; 'Even-colour' is the name of thy father; thou, O plant, producest even colour: render this (spot) of even colour!

4. The black (plant) that produces even colour has been fetched out of the earth. Do thou now, pray, perfect this, construct anew the colours!

VI, 83. Charm for curing scrofulous sores called apakit

1. Fly forth, ye apakit (sores), as an eagle from the nest! Sûrya (the sun) shall prepare a remedy, Kandramâs (the moon) shall shine you away!

2. One is variegated, one is white, one is black, and two are red: I have gotten the names of all of them. Go ye away without slaying men!

3. The apakit, the daughter of the black one, without bearing offspring will fly away; the boil will fly away from here, the galunta (swelling) will perish.

4. Consume thy own (proper) oblation with gratification in thy mind, when I here offer svâhâ in my mind!

VII, 76. A. Charm for curing scrofulous sores called apakit

1. Ye (sores) fall easily from that which falls easily, ye exist less than those that do not exist (at all); ye are drier than the (part of the body called) sehu, more moist than salt.

2. The apakit (sores) that are upon the neck, and those that are upon the shoulders; the apakit that are upon the vigâman (some part of the body) fall off of themselves.

B. Charm for curing tumours called gâyânya

3. The gâyânya that crushes the ribs, that which passes down to the sole of the foot, and whichever is fixed upon the crown of the head, I have driven out every one.

4. The gâyânya, winged, flies; he settles down upon man. Here is the remedy both for sores not caused by cutting as well as for wounds sharply cut!

5. We know, O gâyânya, thy origin, whence thou didst spring. How canst thou slay there, in whose house we offer oblations?

C. Stanza sung at the mid-day pressure of the soma

6. Drink stoutly, O Indra, slayer of Vritra, hero, of the soma in the cup, at the battle for riches! Drink thy fill at the mid-day pressure! Living in wealth, do thou bestow wealth upon us!

VII, 74. A. Charm for curing scrofulous sores called apakit

1. We have heard it said that the mother of the black Apakit (pustules) is red: with the root (found by) the divine sage do I strike all these.

2. I strike the foremost one of them, and I strike also the middlemost of them; this hindmost one I cut off as a flake (of wool).

B. Charm to appease jealousy

3. With Tvashtar's charm I have sobered down thy jealousy; also thy anger, O lord, we have quieted.

C. Prayer to Agni, the lord of vows

4. Do thou, O lord of vows, adorned with vows, ever benevolently here shine! May we all, adoring thee, when thou hast been kindled, O Gâtavedas, be rich in offspring!

VI, 25. Charm against scrofulous sores upon neck and shoulders

1. The five and fifty (sores) that gather together upon the nape of the neck, from here they all shall pass away, as the pustules of the (disease called) apakit!

2. The seven and seventy (sores) that gather together upon the neck, from here they all shall pass away, as the pustules of the (disease called) apakit!

3. The nine and ninety (sores) that gather together upon the shoulders, from here they all shall pass away, as the pustules of the (disease called) apakit!

VI, 57. Urine (gâlâsha) as a cure for scrofulous sores

1. This, verily, is a remedy, this is the remedy of Rudra, with which one may charm away the arrow that has one shaft and a hundred points!

2. With gâlâsha (urine) do ye wash (the tumour), with gâlâsha do ye sprinkle it! The gâlâsha is a potent remedy: do thou (Rudra) with it show mercy to us, that we may live!

3. Both well-being and comfort shall be ours, and nothing whatever shall injure us! To the ground the disease (shall fall): may every remedy be ours, may all remedies be ours!

IV, 12. Charm with the plant arundhatî (lâkshâ) for the cure of fractures

1. Rohan! art thou, causing to heal (rohanî), the broken bone thou causest to heal (rohanî): cause this here to heal (rohaya), O arundhatî!

2. That bone of thine which, injured and burst, exists in thy person, Dhâtar shall kindly knit together again, joint with joint!

3. Thy marrow shall unite with marrow, and thy joint (unite) with joint; the part of thy flesh that has fallen off, and thy bone shall grow together again!

4. Thy marrow shall be joined together with marrow, thy skin grow together with skin! Thy blood, thy bone shall grow, thy flesh grow together with flesh!

5. Fit together hair with hair, and fit together skin with skin! Thy blood, thy bone shall grow: what is cut join thou together, O plant!

6. Do thou here rise up, go forth, run forth, (as) a chariot with sound wheels, firm feloe, and strong nave; stand upright firmly!

7. If he has been injured by falling into a pit, or if a stone was cast and hurt him, may he (Dhâtar, the fashioner) fit him together, joint to joint, as the wagoner (Ribhu) the parts of a chariot!

V, 5. Charm with the plant silâki (lâkshâ, arundhatî) for the cure of wounds

1. The night is thy mother, the cloud thy father, Aryaman thy grandfather. Silâkî, forsooth, is thy name, thou art the sister of the gods.

2. He that drinks thee lives; (that) person thou dost preserve. For thou art the supporter of all successive (generations), the refuge of men.

3. Every tree thou dost climb, like a wench lusting after a man. 'Victorious,' 'firmly founded,' 'saving,' verily, is thy name.

4. The wound that has been inflicted by the club, by the arrow, or by fire, of that thou art the cure: do thou cure this person here!

5. Upon the noble plaksha-tree (ficus infectoria) thou growest up, upon the asvattha (ficus religiosa), the khadira (acacia catechu), and the dhava (grislea tomentosa); (thou growest up) upon the noble nyagrodha (ficus indica, banyan-tree), and the parna (butea frondosa). Come thou to us, O arundhatî!

6. O gold-coloured, lovely, sun-coloured, most handsome (plant), mayest thou come to the fracture, O cure! 'Cure,' verily, is thy name!

7. O gold-coloured, lovely, fiery (plant), with hairy stem, thou art the sister of the waters, O lâkshâ, the wind became thy very breath.

8. Silâkî is thy name, O thou that art brown as a goat, thy father is the son of a maiden. With the blood of the brown horse of Yama thou hast verily been sprinkled.

9. Having dropped from the blood of the horse she ran upon the trees, turning into a winged brook. Do thou come to us, O arundhatî!

VI, 109. The pepper-corn as a cure for wounds

1. The pepper-corn cures the wounds that have been struck by missiles, it also cures the wounds from stabs. Anent it the gods decreed: 'Powerful to secure life this (plant) shall be!'

2. The pepper-corns spake to one another, as they came out, after having been created: 'He whom we shall find (as yet) alive, that man shall not suffer harm!'

3. The Asuras did dig thee into the ground, the gods cast thee up again, as a cure for disease produced by wind (in the body), moreover as a cure for wounds struck by missiles.

I, 17. Charm to stop the flow of blood

1. The maidens that go yonder, the veins, clothed in red garments, like sisters without a brother, bereft of strength, they shall stand still!

2. Stand still, thou lower one, stand still, thou higher one; do thou in the middle also stand still! The most tiny (vein) stands still: may then the great artery also stand still!

Of the hundred arteries, and the thousand veins, those in the middle here have indeed stood still. At the same time the ends have ceased (to flow).

4. Around you has passed a great sandy dike: stand ye still, pray take your case!

II, 31. Charm against worms

1. With Indra's great mill-stone, that crushes all vermin, do I grind to pieces the worms, as lentils with a mill-stone.

2. I have crushed the visible and the invisible worm, and the kurûru, too, I have crushed. All the algandu and the saluna, the worms, we grind to pieces with our charm.

3. The algandu do I smite with a mighty weapon: those that have been burned, and those that have not been burned, have become devoid of strength. Those that are left and those that are not left do I destroy with my song, so that not one of the worms be left.

4. The worm which is in the entrails, and he that is in the head, likewise the one that is in the ribs: avaskava and vyadhvara, the worms, do we crush with (this) charm.

5. The worms that are within the mountains, forests, plants, cattle, and the waters, those that have settled in our bodies, all that brood of the worms do I smite.

II. 32. Charm against worms in cattle

1. The rising sun shall slay the worms, the setting sun with his rays shall slay the worms that are within the cattle!

2. The variegated worm, the four-eyed, the speckled, and the white--I crush his ribs, and I tear off his head.

3. Like Atri, like Kanva, and like Gamadagni do I slay you, ye worms! With the incantation of Agastya do I crush the worms to pieces.

4. Slain is the king of the worms, and their viceroy also is slain. Slain is the worm, with him his mother slain, his brother slain, his sister slain.

5. Slain are they who are inmates with him, slain are his neighbours; moreover all the quite tiny worms are slain.

6. I break off thy two horns with which thou deliverest thy thrusts; I cut that bag of thine which is the receptacle for thy poison.

V, 23. Charm against worms in children

1. I have called upon heaven and earth, I have called upon the goddess Sarasvatî, I have called upon Indra and Agni: 'they shall crush the worm,' (I said).

2. Slay the worms in this boy, O Indra, lord of treasures! Slain are all the evil powers by my fierce imprecation!

3. Him that moves about in the eyes, that moves about in the nose, that gets to the middle of the teeth, that worm do we crush.

4. The two of like colour, the two of different colour; the two black ones, and the two red ones; the brown one, and the brown-eared one; the (one like a) vulture, and the (one like a) cuckoo, are slain.

5. The worms with white shoulders, the black ones with white arms, and all those that are variegated, these worms do we crush.

6. In the east rises the sun, seen by all, slaying that which is not seen; slaying the seen and the unseen (worms), and grinding to pieces all the worms.

7. The yevâsha and the kashkasha, the egatka, and the sipavitnuka--the seen worm shall be slain, moreover the unseen shall be slain!

8. Slain of the worms is the yevâsha, slain further is the nadaniman; all have I crushed down like lentils with a mill-stone.

9. The worm with three heads and the one with three skulls, the speckled, and the white--I crush his ribs and I tear off his head.

10. Like Atri, like Kanva, and like Gamadagni do I slay you, ye worms! With the incantation of Agastya do I crush the worms to pieces.

11. Slain is the king of the worms, and their viceroy also is slain. Slain is the worm, with him his mother slain, his brother slain, his sister slain.

12. Slain are they who are inmates with him, slain are his neighbours; moreover all the quite tiny worms are slain.

13. Of all the male worms, and of all the female worms do I split the heads with the stone, I burn their faces with fire.

IV, 6. Charm against poison

1. The Brâhmana was the first to be born, with ten heads and ten mouths. He was the first to drink the soma; that did render poison powerless.

2. As great as heaven and earth are in extent, as far as the seven streams did spread, so far from here have I proclaimed forth this charm that destroys poison.

3. The eagle Garutmant did, O poison, first devour thee. Thou didst not bewilder him, didst not injure him, yea, thou didst turn into food for him.

4. The five-fingered hand that did hurl upon thee (the arrow) even from the curved bow--from the point of the tearing (arrow) have I charmed away the poison.

5. From the point (of the arrow) have I charmed away the poison, from the substance that has been smeared upon it, and from its plume. From its barbed horn, and its neck, I have charmed away the poison.

6. Powerless, O arrow, is thy point, and powerless is thy poison. Moreover of powerless wood is thy powerless bow, O powerless (arrow)!

7. They that ground (the poison), they that daubed it on, they that hurled it, and they that let it go, all these have been rendered impotent. The mountain that grows poisonous plants has been rendered impotent.

8. Impotent are they that dig thee, impotent art thou, O plant! Impotent is that mountain height whence this poison has sprung.

IV, 7. Charm against poison

1. This water (vâr) in the (river) Varanâvatî shall ward off (vârayâtai)! Amrita (ambrosia) has been poured into it: with that do I ward off (vâraye) poison from thee.

2. Powerless is the poison from the east, powerless that from the north. Moreover the poison from the south transforms itself into a porridge.

3. Having made thee (the poison) that comes from a horizontal direction into a porridge, rich in fat, and cheering, from sheer hunger he has eaten thee, that hast an evil body: do thou not cause injury!

4. Thy bewildering quality (madam), O (plant?) that art bewildering (madivati), we cause to fall like a reed. As a boiling pot of porridge do we remove thee by (our) charm.

5. (Thee, O poison) that art, as it were, heaped about the village, do we cause to stand still by (our) charm. Stand still as a tree upon its place; do not, thou that hast been dug with the spade, cause injury!

6. With broom-straw (?), garments, and also with skins they purchased thee: a thing for barter art thou, O plant! Do not, thou that hast been dug with the spade, cause injury!

7. Those of you who were of yore unequalled in the deeds which they performed-may the), not injure here our men: for this very purpose do I engage you!

VI, 100. Ants as an antidote against poison

1. The gods have given, the sun has given, the earth has given, the three Sarasvatîs, of one mind, have given this poison-destroying (remedy)!

2. That water, O ants, which the gods poured for you into the dry land, with this (water), sent forth by the gods, do ye destroy this poison!

3. Thou art the daughter of the Asuras, thou art the sister of the gods. Sprung from heaven and earth, thou didst render the poison devoid of strength.

VI, 13 Charm against snake-poison

1. Varuna, the sage of heaven, verily lends (power) to rne. With mighty charms do I dissolve thy poison. The (poison) which has been dug, that which has not been dug, and that which is inherent, I have held fast. As a brook in the desert thy poison has dried up.

2. That poison of thine which is not fluid I have confined within these (serpents?). I hold fast the sap that is in thy middle, thy top, and in thy bottom, too. May (the sap) now vanish out of thee from fright!

3. My lusty shout (is) as the thunder with the cloud: then do I smite thy (sap) with my strong charm. With manly strength I have held fast that sap of his. May the sun rise as light from the darkness!

4. With my eye do I slay thy eye, with poison do I slay thy poison. O serpent, die, do not live; back upon thee shall thy poison turn!

5. O kairâta, speckled one, upatrinya (grass-dweller?), brown one, listen to me; ye black repulsive reptiles, (listen to me)! Do not stand upon the ground of my friend; cease with your poison and make it known (to people?)!

6. I release (thee) from the fury of the black serpent, the taimâta, the brown serpent, the poison that is not fluid, the all-conquering, as the bowstring (is loosened) from the bow, as chariots (from horses).

7. Both Âligî and Viligî, both father and mother, we know your kin every-where. Deprived of your strength what will ye do?

8. The daughter of urugûlâ, the evil one born with the black--of all those who have run to their hiding-place the poison is devoid of force.

9. The prickly porcupine, tripping down from the mountain, did declare this: 'Whatsoever serpents, living in ditches, are here, their poison is most deficient in force.'

10. Tâbuvam (or) not tâbuvam, thou (O serpent) art not tâbuvam. Through tâbuvam thy poison is bereft of force.

11. Tastuvam (or) not tastuvam, thou (O serpent) art not tastuvam. Through tastuvarn thy poison is bereft of force.

VI, 12. Charm against snake-poison

1. As the sun (goes around) the heavens I have surrounded the race of the serpents. As night (puts to rest) all animals except the hamsa bird, (thus) do I with this (charm) ward off thy poison.

2. With (the charm) that was found of yore by the Brahmans, found by the Rishis, and found by the gods, with (the charm) that was, will be, and is now present, with this do I ward off thy poison.

3. With honey do I mix the rivers; the mountains and peaks are honey. Honey are the rivers Parushnî and Sîpalâ. Prosperity be to thy mouth, prosperity to thy heart!

VII, 56. Charm against the poison of serpents, scorpions, and insects

1. The poison infused by the serpent that is striped across, by the black serpent, and by the adder; that poison of the kankaparvan ('with limbs like a comb,' scorpion) this plant has driven out.

2. This herb, born of honey, dripping honey, sweet as honey, honied, is the remedy for injuries; moreover it crushes insects.

3. Wherever thou hast been bitten, wherever thou hast been sucked, from there do we exorcise for thee the poison of the small, greedily biting insect, (so that it be) devoid of strength.

4. Thou (serpent) here, crooked, without joints, and without limbs, that twisteth thy crooked jawsmayest thou, O Brihaspati, straighten them out, as

a (bent) reed!
5. The poison of the sarkota (scorpion) that creeps low upon the ground, (after he) has been deprived of his strength, I have taken away; moreover I have caused him to be crushed.

6. There is no strength in thy arms, in thy head, nor in the middle (of thy body). Then why dost thou so wickedly carry a small (sting) in thy tail?

7. The ants devour thee, pea-hens hack thee to pieces. Yea, every one of you shall declare the poison of the sarkota powerless!

8. Thou (scorpion) that strikest with both, with mouth as well as tail, in thy mouth there is no poison: then what can there be in the receptacle in thy tail?

VI, 16. Charm against ophthalmia

1. O âbayu, (and even if) thou art not âbayu, strong is thy juice, O âbayu! We eat a gruel, compounded of thee.

2. Vihalha is thy father's name, Madâvatî thy mother's name. Thou art verily not such, as to have consumed thy own self.

3. O Tauvilikâ, do be quiet! This howling one has become quiet. O brown one, and brown-eared one, go away! Go out, O âla!

4. Alasâlâ thou art first, silâñgalâlâ thou art the next, nîlâgalasâlâ (thou art third?)!

VI, 21. Charm to promote the growth of hair

1. Of these three earths (our) earth verily is the highest. From the surface of these I have now plucked a remedy.

2. Thou art the most excellent of remedies, the best of plants, as Soma (the moon) is the lord in the watches of the night, as Varuna (is king) among the gods.

3. O ye wealthy, irresistible (plants), ye do generously bestow benefits. And ye strengthen the hair, and, moreover, promote its increase.

VI, 136. Charm with the plant nitatni to promote the growth of hair

1. As a goddess upon the goddess earth thou wast born, O plant! We dig thee up, O nitatni, that thou mayest strengthen (the growth) of the hair.

2. Strengthen the old (hair), beget the new! That which has come forth render more luxurious!

3. That hair of thine which does drop off, and that which is broken root and all, upon it do I sprinkle here the all-healing herb.

VI, 137. Charm to promote the growth of hair

1. The (plant) that Gamadagni dug up to promote the growth of his daughter's hair, Vâtahavya has brought here from the dwelling of Asita.

2. With reins they had to be measured, with outstretched arms they had to be measured out. May thy hairs grow as reeds, may they (cluster), black, about thy head!

3. Make firm their roots, draw out their ends, expand their middle., O herb! May thy hairs grow as reeds, may they (cluster), black, about thy head!

IV, 4. Charm to promote virility

1. Thee, the plant, which the Gandharva dug up for Varuna, when his virility had decayed, thee, that causest strength[1], we dig up.

2. Ushas (Aurora), Sûrya, (the sun), and this charm of mine; the bull Pragâpati (the lord of creatures) shall with his lusty fire arouse him!

3. This herb shall make thee so very full of lusty strength, that thou shalt, when thou art excited, exhale heat as a thing on fire!

4. The fire of the plants, and the essence of the bulls shall arouse him! Do thou, O Indra, controller of bodies, place the lusty force of men into this person!

5. Thou (O herb) art the first-born sap of the waters and also of the plants. Moreover thou art the brother of Soma, and the lusty force of the antelope buck!

6. Now, O Agni, now, O Savitar, now, O goddess Sarasvatî, now, O Brahmanaspati, do thou stiffen the pasas as a bow!

7. I stiffen thy pasas as a bowstring upon the bow. Embrace thou (women) as the antelope buck the gazelle with ever unfailing (strength)!

8. The strength of the horse, the mule, the goat and the ram, moreover the strength of the bull bestow upon him, O controller of bodies (Indra)!

[1. The original, more drastically, sepaharshanîm. By a few changes and omissions in stanzas 3, 6, and 7 the direct simplicity of the original has been similarly veiled.]

VI, 111. Charm against mania

1. Release for me, O Agni, this person here, who, bound and well-secured, loudly jabbers! Then shall he have due regard for thy share (of the offering), when he shall be free from madness!

2. Agni shall quiet down thy mind, if it has been disturbed! Cunningly do I prepare a remedy, that thou shalt be freed from madness.

3. (Whose mind) has been maddened by the sin of the gods, or been robbed of sense by the Rakshas, (for him) do I cunningly prepare a remedy, that he shall be free from madness.

4. May the Apsaras restore thee, may Indra, may Bhaga restore thee; may all the gods restore thee, that thou mayest be freed from madness!

IV, 37. Charm with the plant agasringi to drive out Rakshas, Apsaras and Gandharvas

1. With thee, O herb, the Atharvans first slew the Rakshas, with thee Kasyapa slew (them), with thee Kanva and Agastya (slew them).

2. With thee do we scatter the Apsaras and Gandharvas. O agasringi (odina pinnata), goad (aga) the Rakshas, drive them all away with thy smell!

3. The Apsaras, Guggulil, I'lli, Naladi, Aukshagandhi, and Pramandani (by name), shall go to the river, to the ford of the waters, as if blown away! Thither do ye, O Apsaras, pass away, (since) ye have been recognised!

4. Where grow the asvattha (ficus religiosa) and the banyan-trees, the great trees with crowns, thither do ye, O Apsaras, pass away, (since) ye have been recognised!

5. Where your gold and silver swings are, where cymbals and lutes chime together, thither do ye, O Apsaras, pass away, (since) ye have been recog~ nised.

6. Hither has come the mightiest of the plants and herbs. May the agasringi arâtaki pierce with her sharp horn (tîkshmasringî)!

7. Of the crested Gandharva, the husband of the Apsaras, who comes dancing hither, I crush the two mushkas and cut off the sepas.

8. Terrible are the missiles of Indra, with a hundred points, brazen; with these he shall pierce the Gandharvas, who devour oblations, and devour the avakâ-reed.

9. Terrible are the missiles of Indra, with a hundred points, golden; with these he shall pierce the Gandharvas, who devour oblations, and devour the avakd-reed.

10. All the Pisâkas that devour the avakâ-reeds, that burn, and spread their little light in the waters, do thou, O herb, crush and overcome!

11. One is like a dog, one like an ape. As a youth, with luxuriant locks, pleasant to look upon, the Gandharva hangs about the woman. Him do we drive out from here with our powerful charm.

12. The Apsaras, you know, are your wives; ye, the Gandharvas, are their husbands. Speed away, ye immortals, do not go after mortals!

II, 9. Possession by demons of disease, cured by an amulet of ten kinds of wood

1. O (amulet) of ten kinds of wood, release this man from the demon (rakshas) and the fit (grâhi) which has seized upon.(gagrâha) his joints! Do thou, moreover, O plant, lead him forth to the world of the living!

2. He has come, he has gone forth, he has joined the community of the living. And he has become the father of sons, and the most happy of men!

3. This person has come to his senses, he has come to the cities of the living. For he (now) has a hundred physicians, and also a thousand herbs.

4. The gods have found thy arrangement, (O amulet); the Brahmans, moreover, the plants. All the gods have found thy arrangement upon the earth.

5. (The god) that has caused (disease) shall perform the cure; he is himself the best physician.
Let him indeed, the holy one, prepare remedies for thee, together with the (earthly) physician!

IV, 6. Charm against demons (pisâka) conceived as the cause of disease

1. May Agni Vaisvânara, the bull of unfailing strength, burn up him that is evil-disposed, and desires to harm us, and him that plans hostile deeds against us!

2. Between the two rows of teeth of Agni Vaisvânara do I place him that plans to injure us, when we are not planning to injure him; and him that plans to injure us, when we do plan to injure him.

Those who hound us in our chambers, while shouting goes on in the night of the new moon, and the other flesh-devourers who plan to injure us, all of them do I overcome with might.

4. With might I overcome the Pisâkas, rob them of their property; all evil-disposed (demons) do I slay: may my device succeed!

5. With the gods who vie with, and measure their swiftness with this sun, with those that are in the rivers, and in the mountains, do I, along with my cattle, consort.

6. I plague the Pisâkas as the tiger the cattle-owners. As dogs who have seen a lion, these do not find a refuge.

7. My strength does not lie with Pisâkas, nor with thieves, nor with prowlers in the forest. From the village which I enter the Pisâkas vanish away.

8. From the village which my fierce power has entered the Pisâkas vanish away; they do not devise evil.

9. They who irritate me with their jabber, as (buzzing) mosquitoes the elephant, them I regard as wretched (creatures), as small vermin upon people.

10. May Nirriti (the goddess of destruction) take hold of this one, as a horse with the halter! The fool who is wroth with me is not freed from (her) snare.

II, 25. Charm with the plant prisniparnî against the demon of disease, called kanva

1. The goddess Prisniparnî has prepared prosperity for us, mishap for Nirriti (the goddess of destruction). For she is a fierce devourer of the Kanvas: her, the mighty, have I employed.

2. The Prisniparnî was first begotten powerful; with her do I lop off the heads of the evil brood, as (the head) of a bird.

3. The blood-sucking demon, and him that tries to rob (our) health, Kanva, the devourer of our offspring, destroy, O Prisniparnî, and overcome!

4. These Kanvas, the effacers of life, drive into the mountain; go thou burning after them like fire, O goddess Prisniparnî!

5. Drive far away these Kanvas, the effacers of life! Where the dark regions are, there have I made these flesh-eaters go.

VI, 32. Charm for driving away demons (Rakshas and Pisâkas)

1. Do ye well offer within the fire this oblation with ghee, that destroys the spook! Do thou, O Agni, burn from afar against the Rakshas, (but) our houses thou shalt not consume!

2. Rudra has broken your necks, ye Pisâkas: may he also break your ribs, ye spooks! The plant whose power is everywhere has united you with Yama (death).

3. Exempt from danger, O Mitra and Varuna, may we here be; drive back with your flames the devouring demons (Atrin)! Neither aider, nor support do they find; smiting one another they go to death.

II, 4. Charm with an amulet derived from the gangida tree, against diseases and demons

1. Unto long life and great delights, for ever unharmed and vigorous, do we wear the gangida, as an amulet destructive of the vishkandha.

2. From convulsions, from tearing pain, from vishkandha, and from torturing pain, the gangida shall protect us on all sides--an amulet of a thousand virtues!

3. This gangida conquers the vishkandha, and smites the Atrin (devouring demons); may this all-healing gangida protect us from adversity!

4. By means of the invigorating gangida, bestowed by the gods as an amulet, do we conquer in battle the vishkandha and all the Rakshas.

5. May the hemp and may gangida protect me against vishkandha! The one (gangida) is brought hither from the forest, the other (hemp) from the sap of the furrow.

6. Destruction of witchcraft is this amulet, also destruction of hostile powers: may the powerful gangida therefore extend far our lives!

XIX, 34, Charm with an amulet derived from the gafigpida-tree, aoainst diseases and demons

1. Thou art an Angiras, O gangida, a protector art thou, O gangida. All two-footed and four-footed creatures that belong to us the gangida shall protect!

2. The sorceries fifty-three in number, and the hundred performers of sorcery, all these having lost their force, the gangida shall render bereft of strength!

3. Bereft of strength is the gotten-up clamour, bereft of strength are the seven debilitating (charms). Do thou, O gangida, hurl away from here poverty, as an archer an arrow!

4. This gangida is a destroyer of witchcraft, and also a destroyer of hostile powers. May then the powerful gangida extend far our lives!

5. May the greatness of the gangida protect us about on all sides, (the greatness) with which he has overcome the vishkandha (and) the sams-kandha, (overcoming the powerful (disease) with power!

6. Thrice the gods begot thee that hast grown up upon the earth. The Brahmanas of yore knew thee here by the name of Angiras.

7. Neither the plants of olden times, nor they of recent times, surpass thee; a fierce slayer is the gahaida, and a happy refuge.

8 And when, O gangida of boundless virtue, thou didst spring up in the days of yore, O fierce (plant), Indra at first placed strength in thee.

9. Fierce Indra, verily, put might into thee, O lord of the forest! Dispersing all diseases, slay thou the Rakshas, O plant!

I o. The breaking disease and the tearing disease, the balâsa, and the pain in the limbs, the takman that comes every autumn, may the gangida render devoid of force!

XIX, 35. Charm with an amulet derived from the gangida-tree, against diseases and demons

1. While uttering Indra's name the seers bestowed (upon men) the gangida, which the gods in the beginning had made into a remedy, destructive of the vishkandha.

2 . May that gangida protect us as a treasurer his treasures, he whom the gods and the Brâhmanas made into a refuge that puts to naught the hostile powers!

3. The evil eye of the hostile-minded, (and) the evil-doer I have approached. Do thou, O thousandeyed one, watchfully destroy these! A refuge art thou, O gangida.

4. May the gangida protect me from heaven, protect me from earth, protect (me) from the atmosphere, protect me from the plants, protect me from the past, as well as the future; may he protect us from every direction of space!

5. The sorceries performed by the gods, and also those performed by men, may the all-healing gangida render them all devoid of strength!

VI, 85. Exorcism of disease by means of an amulet from the varana-tree

1. This divine tree, the varana, shall shut out (vârayâtai). The gods, too, have shut out (avîvaran) the disease that hath entered into this man!

2. By Indra's command, by Mitra's and by Varuna's, by the command of all the gods do we shut out thy disease.

3. As Vritra did bold fast these ever-flowing waters, thus do I shut out (vâraye) disease from thee with (the help of) Agni Vaisvânara.

VI, 127. The kîpudru-tree as a panacea

1. Of the abscess, of the balâsa, of flow of blood, O plant; of neuralgia, O herb, thou shalt not leave even a speck!

2. Those two boils (testicles) of thine, O balasa, that are fixed upon the arm-pits-I know the remedy for that: the kîpudru-tree takes care of it.

3. The neuralgia that is in the limbs, that is in the ears and in the eyes-we tear them out, the neuralgia, the abscess, and the pain in the heart. That unknown disease do we drive away downward.

XIX, 38. The healing properties of bdellium

1. [Neither diseases, nor yet a curse, enters this person, O arundhatî!] From him that is penetrated by the sweet fragrance of the healing bdellium, diseases flee in every direction, as antelopes and as horses run.

2. Whether, O bdellium, thou comest from the Sindhu (Indus), or whether thou art derived from the sea, I have seized the qualities of both, that this person shall be exempt from harm.

VI, 91. Barley and water as universal remedies

1. This barley they did plough vigorously, with yokes of eight and yokes of six. With it I drive off to a far distance the ailment from thy body.

2. Downward blows the wind, downward burns the sun, downward the cow is milked: downward shall thy ailment pass!

3. The waters verily are healing, the waters chase away disease, the waters cure all (disease): may they prepare a remedy for thee!

VIII, 7. Hymn to all magic and medicinal plants, used as a universal remedy

1. The plants that are brown, and those that are white; the red ones and the speckled ones; the sable and the black plants, all (these) do we invoke.

2. May they protect this man from the disease sent by the gods, the herbs whose father is the sky, whose mother is the earth, whose root is the ocean.

3. The waters and the heavenly plants are foremost; they have driven out from every limb thy disease, consequent upon sin.

4. The plants that spread forth, those that are busby, those that have a single sheath, those that creep along, do I address; I call in thy behalf the plants that have shoots, those that have stalks, those that divide their branches, those that are derived from all the gods, the strong (plants) that furnish

life to man.

5. With the might that is yours, ye mighty ones, with the power and strength that is yours, with that do ye, O plants, rescue this man from this disease!

I now prepare a remedy.
6. The plants givalâ ('quickening'), na-ghâ-rishâ ('forsooth-no-harm'), gîvanti ('living'), and the arundhatî, which removes (disease), is full of blossoms, and rich in honey, do I call to exempt him from injury.

7. Hither shall come the intelligent (plants) that understand my speech, that we may bring this man into safety out of misery!

8. They that are the food of Agni (the fire), the offspring of the waters, that grow ever renewing themselves, the firm (plants) that bear a thousand names, the healing (plants), shall be brought hither!

9. The plants, whose womb is the avaki (blyxa octandra), whose essence are the waters, shall with their sharp horns thrust aside evil!

10. The plants which release, exempt from Varuna (dropsy), are strong, and destroy poison; those, too, that remove (the disease) baldsa, and ward off witchcraft shall come hither!'

11. The plants that have been bought, that are right potent, and are praised, shall protect in this village cow, horse, man, and cattle!

12. Honied are the roots of these herbs, honied their tops, honied their middles, honied their leaves, honied their blossoms; they share in honey, are the food of immortality. May they yield ghee, and food, and cattle chief of all!

13. As many in number and in kind the plants here are upon the earth, may they, furnished with a thousand leaves, release me from death and misery!

14. Tiger-like is the amulet (made of) herbs, a saviour, a protector against hostile schemes: may it drive off far away from us all diseases and the Rakshas!

15. As if at the roar of the lion they start with fright, as if (at the roar) of fire they tremble before the (plants) that have been brought hither. The

diseases of cattle and men have been driven out by the herbs: let them pass into navigable streams!

16. The plants release us from Agni Vaisvânara. Spreading over the earth, go ye, whose king is the tree!

17. The plants, descended from Angiras, that grow upon the mountains and in the plains, shall be for us rich in milk, auspicious, comforting to the heart!

18. The herbs which I know, and those which I see with my sight; the unknown, those which we know, and those which we perceive to be charged with (power),--

19. All plants collectively shall note my words, that we may bring this man into safety out of misfortune,--

20. The asvattha (ficus religiosa), and the darbha among the plants; king Soma, amrita (ambrosia) and the oblation; rice and barley, the two healing, immortal children of heaven!

21. Ye arise: it is thundering and crashing, ye plants, since Parganya (the god of rain) is favouring you, O children of Prisni (the spotted cloud), with (his) seed (water).

22. The strength of this amrita (ambrosia) do we crive this man to drink. Moreover, I prepare a remedy, that he may live a hundred years!

23. The boar knows, the ichneumon knows the healing plant. Those that the serpents and Gandharvas know, I call hither for help.

24. The plants, derived from the Angiras, which the eagles and the heavenly raghats (falcons) know, which the birds and the flamingos know, which all winged (creatures) know, which all wild animals know, I call hither for help.

25. As many plants as the oxen and kine, as many as the goats and the sheep feed upon, so many plants, when applied, shall furnish protection to thee!

26. As many (plants), as the human physicians know to contain a remedy, so many, endowed with every healing quality, do I apply to thee!

27. Those that have flowers, those that have blossoms, those that bear fruit, and those that are without fruit, as if from the same mother they shall suck sap, to exempt this man from injury!

28. I have saved thee from a depth of five fathoms, and, too, from a depth of ten fathoms; moreover, from the foot-fetter of Yama, and from every sin against the gods.

VI, 96. Plants as a panacea

1. The many plants of hundredfold aspect, whose king is Soma, which have been begotten by Brihaspati, shall free us from calamity!

2. May they free us from (the calamity) consequent upon curses, and also from the (toils) of Varuna; moreover, from the foot-fetter of Yama, and every sin against the gods!

3. What laws we have infringed upon, with the eye, the mind, and speech, either while awake, or asleep-may Soma by his (divine) nature clear these (sins) away from us!

II, 32. Charm to secure perfect health

1. From thy eyes, thy nostrils, ears, and chin--the disease which is seated in thy head--from thy brain and tongue I do tear it out.

2. From thy neck, nape of the neck, ribs, and spine--the disease which is seated in thy fore-arm--from thy shoulders and arms I do tear it out.

3. From thy heart, thy lungs, viscera, and sides; from thy kidneys, spleen, and liver we do tear out the disease.

4. From thy entrails, canals, rectum, and abdomen; from thy belly, guts, and navel I do tear out the disease.

5. From thy thighs, knees, heels, and the tips of thy feet--from thy hips I do tear out the disease seated in thy buttocks, from thy bottom the disease seated in thy buttocks.

6. From thy bones, marrow, sinews and arteries; from thy hands, fingers, and nails I do tear out the disease.

7. The disease that is in thy every limb, thy every hair, thy every joint; that which is seated in thy skin, with Kasyapa's charm, that tears out, to either side we do tear it out.

IX, 8. Charm to procure immunity from all diseases

1. Headache and suffering in the head, pain in the ears and flow of blood, every disease of the head, do we charm forth from thee.

2. From thy ears, from thy kankûshas the earpain, and the neuralgia--every disease of the head do we charm forth from thee.

3. (With the charm) through whose agency disease hastens forth from the ears and the mouth-every disease of the head do we charm forth from thee.

4. (The disease) that renders a man deaf and blind--every disease of the head do we charm forth from thee.

5. Pain in the limbs, fever in the limbs, the neuralgia that affects every limb-every disease of the head do we charm forth from thee.

6. (The disease) whose frightful aspect makes man tremble, the takman (fever) that comes every autumn, do we charm forth from thee.

7. The disease that creeps along the thighs, and then enters the canals, out of thy inner parts do we charm forth.

8. If from the heart, from love, or from disgust, it arises, from thy heart and from thy limbs the balâsa do we charm forth.

9. Jaundice from thy limbs, diarrhoea from within thy bowels, the core of disease from thy inner soul do we charm forth.

10. To ashes (âsa) the balâsa shall turn; what is diseased shall turn to urine! The poison of all diseases I have charmed forth from thee.

11. Outside the opening (of the bladder) it shall run off; the rumbling shall pass from thy belly! The poison of all diseases I have charmed forth from thee.

12. From thy belly, lungs, navel, and heart-the poison of all diseases I have charmed forth from thee.

13. (The pains) that split the crown (of the head), pierce the head, without doing injury, without causing disease, they shall run off outside the opening (of the bladder)!

14. They that pierce the heart, creep along the ribs, without doing injury, without causing disease, they shall run off outside the opening (of the bladder)!

15. They that pierce the sides, bore along the ribs, without doing injury, without causing disease, they shall run off outside the opening (of the bladder)!

16. They that pierce crosswise, burrow in thy abdomen, without doing injury, without causing disease, they shall run off outside the opening (of the bladder)!

17. They that creep along the rectum, twist the bowels, without doing injury, without causing disease, they shall run off outside the opening (of the bladder)!

18. They that suck the marrow, and split the joints, without doing injury, without causing disease, they shall run off outside the opening (of the bladder)!

19. The diseases and the injuries that paralyse thy limbs, the poison of all diseases I have charmed forth from thee.

20. Of neuralgia, of abscesses, of inflation, or of inflammation of the eyes, the poison of all diseases I have driven forth from thee.

21. From thy feet, knees, thighs, and bottom; from thy spine, and thy neck the piercing pains, from thy head the ache I have removed.

22. Firm are the bones of thy skull, and the beat of thy heart. At thy rising, O sun, thou didst remove the pains of the head, quiet the pangs in the limbs.

II, 29. Charm for obtaining long life and prosperity by transmission of disease

1. In the essence of earthly bliss, O ye gods, in strength of body (may he live)! May Agni, Sûrya, Brihaspati bestow upon him life's vigour!

2. Give life to him, O Gâtavedas, bestow in addition progeny upon him, O Tvashtar; procure, O Savitar, increase of wealth for him; may this one, who belongs to thee, live a hundred autumns!

3. May our prayer bestow upon us vigour, and possession of sound. progeny; ability and property do ye two, (O heaven and earth), bestow upon us!, May he, conquering lands with might, (live), O Indra, subjecting the others, his enemies!

4. Given by Indra, instructed by Varuna, sent by the Maruts, strong, he has come to us; may he, in the lap of ye two, heaven and earth, not suffer from hunger and not from thirst!

5. Strength may ye two, that are rich in strength, bestow upon him; milk may ye two, that are rich in milk, bestow upon him! Strength heaven and earth did bestow upon him; strength all the gods, the Maruts, and the waters.

6. With the gracious (waters) do I delight thy heart, mayest thou, free from disease, full of force, rejoice! Clothed in the same garment do ye two drink this stirred drink, taking on as a magic form the shape of the two Asvins!

7. Indra, having been wounded, first created this vigour, and this ever fresh divine food: that same belongs to thee. By means of that do thou, full of force, live (a hundred) autumns; may it not flow out of thee: physicians have prepared it for thee!

PRAYERS FOR LONG LIFE AND HEALTH (ÂYU-SHYÂNI)

III, 11. Prayer for health and long life

1. I release thee unto life by means of (my) oblation, from unknown decline, and from consumption. If Grâhi (seizure) has caught hold (gagrâha) of this person here, may Indra and Agni free him from that!

2. If his life has faded, even if he has passed away, if he has been brought to the very vicinity of death, I snatch him from the lap of Nirriti (the goddess of destruction): I have freed him unto a life of a hundred autumns.

3. I have snatched him (from death) by means of an oblation which has a thousand eyes, hundredfold strength, and -ensures a hundredfold life, in order that Indra may conduct him through the years across to the other side of every misfortune.

4. Live thou, thriving a hundred autumns, a hundred winters, and a hundred springs! May Indra, Agni, Savitar, Brihaspati (grant) thee a hundred years! I have snatched him (from death) with an oblation that secures a life,of a hundred years.

5. Enter ye, O in-breathirig and out-breathing, as two bulls a stable! Away shall go the other deaths, of which, it is said, there are a hundred more!

6. Remain ye here, O in-breathing and out-breathing, do not go away from here; do ye car anew to old age his body and his limbs!

7. To old age I make thee over, into old age I urge thee; may a happy old age guide thee! Away shall go the other deaths, of which, it is said, there are a hundred more!

8. Upon thee (life unto) old age has been deposited, as a rope is tied upon a bull. That death which has fettered thee at thy birth with a firm rope, Brihaspati with the hands of the truth did strip off from thee.

II, 28. Prayer for long life pronounced over a boy

1. For thee alone, O (death from) old age, this (boy) shall grow up: the other hundred kinds of death shall not harm him! Like a provident mother in her lap Mitra shall befriend him, shall save him from misfortune!

2. May Mitra or Varuna, the illustrious, cooperating, grant him death from old age! Then Agni, the priest, who knows the ways, promulgates all the races of the gods.

3. Thou, (O Agni), rulest over all the animals of the earth, those which have been born, and those which are to be born: may not in-breathing leave this one, nor yet out-breathing, may neither friends nor foes slay him!

4. May father Dyaus (sky) and mother Prithivi (earth), co-operating, grant thee death from old age, that thou mayest live in the lap of Aditi a hundred winters, guarded by in-breathing and outbreathing!

5. Lead this dear child to life and vigour, O Agni, Varuna, and king Mitra! As a mother afford him protection, O Aditi, and all ye gods, that he may attain to old age!

III, 31. Prayer for health and long life

1. The gods are free from decrepitude; thou, O Agni, art removed from the demon of hostility. I free thee from all evil and disease, (and) unite thee with life.

2. (Vâyu), the purifying (wind), shall free thee from misfortune, Sakra (Indra) from evil sorcery! I free thee from all evil and disease, (and) unite thee with life.

3. The tame (village) animals are separate from the wild (forest animals); the water has flowed apart from thirst. I free thee from all evil and disease, (and) unite thee with life.

4. Heaven and earth here go apart; the paths go in every direction. I free thee from all evil and disease, (and) unite thee with life.

5. 'Tvashtar is preparing a wedding for his daughter,' thus (saying) does this whole world pass through. I free thee from all evil and disease, (and) unite thee with life.

6. Agni unites (life's) breaths, the moon is united with (life's) breath. I free thee from all evil and disease, (and) unite thee with life.

7. By means of (life's) breath the gods aroused the everywhere mighty sun. I free thee from all evil and disease, (and) unite thee with life.

8. Live thou by the (life's) breath of them that have life, and that create life; do not die! I free thee from all evil and disease, (and) unite thee with life.

9. Breathe thou with the (life's) breath of those that breathe; do not die! I free thee from all evil and disease, (and) unite thee with life.

10. Do thou (rise) up with life, unite thyself with life, (rise) up with the sap of the plants! I free thee from all evil and disease, (and) unite thee with life.

11. From the rain of Parganya we have risen up, immortal. I free thee from all evil and disease, (and) unite thee with life.

VII, 53. Prayer for long life

1. When, O Brihaspati, thou didst liberate (us) from existence in yonder world of Yama, (and) from hostile schemes, then did the Asvins, the physicians of the gods, with might sweep death from us, O Agni!

2. O in-breathing and out-breathing, go along with the body, do not leave it: may they be thy allies here! Live and thrive a hundred autumns; Agni shall be thy most excellent shepherd and overseer!

3. Thy vital force that has been dissipated afar, thy in-breathing and thy out-breathing, shall come back again! Agni has snatched them from the lap of Nirriti (the goddess of destruction), and I again introduce them into thy person.

4. Let not his in-breathing desert him, nor his out-breathing quit him and depart! I commit him to the Seven Rishis: may they convey him in health to old age!

5. Enter, O in-breathing and out-breathing, like two bulls into a stable: this person shall here flourish, an unmolested repository for old age!

6. Life's breath we do drive into thee, disease we do drive away from thee. May this excellent Agni endow us with life from every source!

7. Ascending from the darkness of death to the highest firmament, to Sûrya (the sun), the god among gods, we have reached the highest light.

VIII, 1. Prayer for exemption from the dangers of death

1. To the 'Ender,' to Death be reverence! May thy in-breathing and thy out-breathing remain here! United here with (life's) spirit this man shall be, sharing in the sun, in the world of immortality (amrita)!

2. Bhaga has raised him up, Soma with his rays (has raised) him up, the Maruts, the gods, (have raised) him up, Indra and Agni (have raised) him up unto well-being.

3. Here (shall be) thy (life's) spirit, here thy inbreathing, here thy life, here thy mind! We rescue thee from the toils of Nirriti (destruction) by means of our divine utterance.

4. Rise up hence, O man! Casting off the footshackles of death, do not sink down! Be not cut off from this world, from the sight of Agni and the sun!

5. The wind, Mâtarisvan, shall blow for thee, the waters shall shower amrita (ambrosia) upon thee, the sun shall shine kindly for thy body! Death shall pity thee: do not waste away!

6. Thou shalt ascend and not descend, O man! Life and alertness do I prepare for thee. Mount, forsooth, this imperishable, pleasant car; then in old age thou shalt hold converse with thy family!

7. Thy mind shall not go thither, shall not disappear! Do not become heedless of the living, do not follow the Fathers! All the gods shall preserve thee here!

8. Do not long after the departed, who conduct (men) afar! Ascend from the darkness, come to the light! We lay hold of thy hands.

9. The two dogs of Yama, the black and the brindled one, that guard the road (to heaven), that have been despatched, shall not (go after) thee! Come hither, do not long to be away; do not tarry here with thy mind turned to a distance!

10. Do not follow this path: it is terrible! I speak of that by which thou hast not hitherto gone. Darkness is this, O man, do not enter it! Danger is beyond, security here for thee.

11. May the fires that are within the waters gLiard thee, may (the fire) which men kindle guard thee, may Gâtavedas Vaisvânara (the fire common to all men) guard thee! Let not the heavenly (fire) together with the lightning burn, thee!

12. Let not the flesh-devouring (fire) menace thee: move afar from the funeral pyre! Heaven shall guard thee, the earth shall guard thee, the sun and moon shall guard thee, the atmosphere shall guard thee against the divine missile!

13. May the alert and the watchful divinities guard thee, may he that sleeps not and nods not guard thee, may he that protects and is vigilant guard thee!

14. They shall guard thee, they shall protect thee. Reverence be to them. Hail be to them!
15. Into converse with the living Vâyu, Indra, Dhâtar, and saving Savitar shall put thee; breath and strength shall not leave thee! Thy (life's) spirit do we call back to thee.

16. Convulsions that draw the jaws together, darkness, shall not come upon thee, nor (the demon) that tears out the tongue (?)! How shalt thou then waste away? The Âdityas and Vasus, Indra and Agni shall raise thee up unto well-being!

17. The heavens, the earth, Pragâpati, have rescued thee. The plants with Soma their king have delivered thee from death.

18. Let this man remain right here, ye gods, let him not depart hence to yonder world! We rescue him from death with (a charm) of thousandfold strength.

19. I have delivered thee from death. The (powers) that furnish strength shall breathe upon thee. The (mourning women) with dishevelled hair, they that wail lugubriously, shall not wail over thee!

20. I have snatched thee (from death), I have obtained thee; thou hast returned with renewed youth. O thou, that art (now) sound of limb, for thee sound sight, and sound life have I obtained.

21. It has shone upon thee, light has arisen, darkness has departed from thee. We remove from thee death, destruction, and disease.

VIII, 2. Prayer for exemption from the dangers of death

1. Take hold of this (charm) that subjects to immortality (life), may thy life unto old age not be cut off! I bring to thee anew breath and life: not to mist and darkness, do not waste away!

2. Come hither to the light of the living; I rescue thee unto a life of a hundred autumns! Loosing the bands of death and imprecation, I bestow upon thee long life extended very far.

3. From the wind thy breath I have obtained, from the sun thine eye; thy soul I hold fast in thee: be together with thy limbs, speak articulating with thy tongue!

4. With the breath of two-footed and four-footed creatures I blow upon thee, as on Agni when he is born (as on fire when kindled). I have paid reverence, O death, to thine eye, reverence to thy breath.

5. This (man) shall live and shall not die: we rouse this man (to life)! I make for him a remedy: O death, do not slay the man!

6. The plant gîvalâ (quickening'), na-ghâ-rishâ ('forsooth-no-harm'), and gîvantî ('living), a victorious, mighty saviour-plant do I invoke, that he may be exempt from injury.

7. Befriend him, do not seize him, let him go, (O death); though he be thy very own, let him abide here with unimpaired strength! O Bhava and Sarva, take pity, grant Protection; misfortune drive away, and life bestow!

8. Befriend him, death, and pity him: may he from here arise! Unharmed, with sound limbs, hearing perfectly, through old age carrying a hundred years, let him get enjoyment by himself (unaided)!

9. The missile of the gods shall pass thee by! I pass thee across the mist (of death); from death I have rescued thee. Removing far the flesh-devouring Agni, a barrier do I set around thee, that thou mayest live.

10. From thy misty road that cannot be withstood, O death, from this path (of thine) we guard this (man), and make our charm a protection for him.

11. In-breathing and out-breathing. do I prepare for thee, death in old age, long life, and prosperity. All the messengers of Yama, that roam about, dispatched by Vivasvant's son, do I drive away.

12. Arâti (grudge), Nirriti (destruction), Grâhi (seizure), and the flesh-devouring Pisâkas (do we drive) away to a distance, and hurl all wicked Rakshas away into darkness as it were.

13. I crave thy life's breath from the immortal, life-possessing Agni Gâtavedas. That thou shalt not take harm, shalt be immortal in (Agni's) company, that do I procure for thee, and that shall be fulfilled for thee!

14. May heaven and earth, the bestowers of happiness, be auspicious and harmless to thee; may the sun-shine, and the wind blow comfort to thy heart; may the heavenly waters, rich in milk, flow upon thee kindly!

15. May the plants be auspicious to thee! I have raised thee from the lower to the upper earth: there may both the Âdityas, the sun and the moon, . protect thee.

16. Whatever garment for clothing, or whatever girdle thou makest for thyself, agreeable to thy body do we render it; not rough to thy touch shall it be!

17. When thou, the barber, shearest with thy sharp well-whetted razor our hair and beard, do not, while cleansing our face, rob us of our life!

18. Rice and barley shall be auspicious to thee, causing no balâsa, inflicting no injury! They two drive away disease, they two release from calamity.

19. Whatever thou eatest or drinkest, the grain of the plough-land or milk, whatever is or is not to be eaten, all that food do I render for thee free from poison.

20. To day and to night both do we commit thee: from the demons that seek to devour, do ye preserve this (man) for me!

21. A hundred years, ten thousand years, two, three, four ages (yuga) do we allot to thee; Indra and Agni, and all the gods without anger shall favour thee!

22. To autumn thee, to winter, spring and summer, do we commit; the rains in which grow the plants shall be pleasant to thee!

23. Death rules over bipeds, death rules over quadrupeds. From that death, the lord of cattle, do I rescue thee: do not fear!

24. Free from harm thou shalt not die; thou shalt not die: do not fear! Verily, they do not die there, they do not go to the nethermost darkness;--

25. Verily, every creature lives there, the cow, the horse, and man, where this charm is performed, as the (protecting) barrier for life.

26. May it preserve thee from sorcery, from thy equals and thy kin! Undying be, immortal, exceedingly vital; thy spirits shall not abandon thy body!

27. From the one and a hundred deaths, from the dangers that are surmountable, from that Agai Vaisvânara (the funeral pyre?) may the gods deliver thee!

28. Thou, the remedy called p6tudru, art the body of Agni, the deliverer, slayer of Rakshas, slayer of rivals, moreover thou chasest away disease.

V. 30. Prayer for exemption from disease and death

1. From near thy vicinity, from near thy distance (do I call): remain here, do not follow; do not follow the Fathers of yore! Firmly do I fasten thy life's breath.

2. Whatever sorcery any kinsman or stranger has practised against thee, both release and deliverance with my voice do I declare for thee.

3. If thou hast deceived or cursed a woman or a man in thy folly, both release and deliverance with my voice do I declare for thee.

4. If thou liest (ill) in consequence of a sin committed by thy mother or thy father, both release and deliverance with my voice do I declare for thee.

5. Fight shy of the medicine which thy mother and thy father, thy sister and thy brother let out against thee: I shall cause thee to live unto old age!

6. Remain here, O man, with thy entire soul; do not follow the two messengers of Yama: come to the abodes of the living!

7. Return when called, knowing the outlet of the path (death), the ascent, the advance, the road of every living man!

8. Fear not, thou shalt not die: I shall cause thee to live unto old age! I have charmed away from thy limbs the disease that wastes the limbs.

9. The disease that racks and wastes thy limbs, and the sickness in thy heart, has flown as an eagle to a far distance, overcome by my charm.

10. The two sages Alert and Watchful, the sleepless and the vigilant, these two guardians of thy life's breath, are awake both day and night.

11. Agni here is to be revered; the sun shall rise here for thee: rise thou from deep death, yea from black darkness!

12. Reverence be to Yama, reverence to death; reverence to the Fathers and to those that lead (to them) [death's messengers?]! That Agni who knows the way to save do I engage for this man, that he be exempt from harm!

13. His breath shall come, his soul shall come, his sight shall come, and, too, his strength! His body shall collect itself: then shall he stand firm upon his feet!

14. Unite him, Agni, with breath and sight, provide him with a body and with strength! Thou hast a knowledge of immortality: let him not now depart, let him not now become a dweller in a house of clay!

15. Thy in-breathing shall not cease, thy outbreathing shall not vanish; Sûrya (the sun), the supreme lord, shall raise thee from death with his rays!

16. This tongue (of mine), bound (in the mouth, yet) mobile, speaks within: with it I have charmed away disease, and the hundred torments of the takman (fever).

17. This world is most dear to the gods, unconquered. For whatever death thou wast destined when thou wast born, O man, that (death) and we call after thee: do not die before old age!

IV, 9. Salve (âñgana) as a protector of life and limb

1. Come hither! Thou art the living, protecting eye-ointment of the mountain, given by all the gods as a safeguard, unto life.

2. Thou art a protection for men, a protection for cattle, thou didst stand for the protection of horses and steeds.

3. Thou art, O salve, both a protection that crushes the sorcerers, and thou hast knowledge of immortality (amrita). Moreover, thou art food for the living, and thou art, too, a remedy aorainst jaundice.

4. From him over whose every limb and every joint thou passest, O salve, thou dost, as a mighty intercepter, drive away disease.

5. Him that bears thee, O salve, neither curse, nor sorcery, nor burning pain does reach; nor does the,vishkandha come upon him.

6. From evil scheme, from troubled dream, from evil deed, and also from foulness.; from the evil eye of the enemy, from this protect us, O salve!

7. Knowing this, O salve, I shall speak the truth, avoid falsehood. May I obtain horses and cattle, and thy person, O serving-man!

8. Three are servants of the salve: the takman (fever), the balâsa, and the serpent. The highest of the mountains, Trikakud ('Three-peaks') by name, is thy father.

9. Since the salve of Trikakud is born upon the Himavant, it shall demolish all the wizards and all the witches.

10. Whether thou art derived from the (mountain) Trikakud, or art said to come from the (river) Yamunâ, both these names of thine are auspicious: with these, O salve, protect us!

IV, 10. The pearl and its shell as an amulet bestowing long life and prosperity

1. Born of the wind, the atmosphere, the lightning, and the light, may this pearl shell, born of gold, protect us from straits!

2. With the shell which was born in the sea, at the head of bright substances, we slay the Rakshas and conquer the Atrins (devouring demons).

3. With the shell (we conquer) disease and poverty; with the shell, too, the Saânvâs. The shell is our universal remedy; the pearl shall protect us from straits!

4. Born in the heavens, born in the sea, brought on from the river (Sindhu), this shell, born of gold, is our life-prolonging amulet.

5. The amulet, born from the sea, a sun, born from Vritra (the cloud), shall on all sides protect us from the missiles of the gods and the Asuras!

6. Thou art one of the golden substances, thou art born from Soma (the moon). Thou art sightly on the chariot, thou art brilliant on the quiver. [May it prolong our lives!]

7. The bone of the gods turned into pearl; that, animated, dwells in the waters. That do I fasten upon thee unto life, lustre, strength, longevity,

unto a life lasting a hundred autumns, May the (amulet) of pearl protect thee!

XIX, 26. Gold as an amulet for long life

1. The gold which is born from fire, the immortal, they bestowed upon the mortals. He who knows this deserves it; of old age dies he who wears it.

2. The gold, (endowed by) the sun with beautiful colour, which the men of yore, rich in descendants, did desire, may it gleaming envelop thee in lustre! Long-lived becomes he who wears it!

3. (May it envelop) thee unto (long) life, unto lustre, unto force, and unto strength, that thou shalt by the brilliancy of the gold shine forth among people!

4. (The gold) which king Varuna knows, which god Brihaspati knows, which Indra, the slayer of Vritra, knows, may that become for thee a source of life, may that become for thee a source of lustre!

IMPRECATIONS AGAINST DEMONS, SORCERERS, AND ENEMIES (ÂBHIKÂRIKÂNI AND KRITYÂPRATIHA-RANÂNI)

I, 7. Against sorcerers and demons

1. The sorcerer (yâtudhâna) that vaunts himsel and the Kimîdin do thou, O Agni, convey hither! For thou, O god, when lauded, becomest the destroyer of the demon.

2. Partake of the ghee, of the sesame-oil, O Agni Gâtavedas, that standest on high, conquerest by thyself! Make the sorcerers howl!

3. The sorcerers and the devouring (atrin) Kimîdin shall howl! Do ye, moreover, O Agni and Indra, receive graciously this our oblation!

4. Agni shall be the first to seize them, Indra with his (strong) arms shall drive them away! Every wizard, as soon as he comes, shall proclaim himself, saying, 'I am he'!

5. We would see thy might, O Gâtavedas; disclose to us the wizards, O thou that beholdest men! May they all, driven forth by thy fire, disclosing themselves, come to this spot!

6. Seize hold, O Gâtavedas: for our good thou wast born! Become our messenger, O Agni, and make the sorcerers howl!

7. Do thou, O Agni, drag hither the sorcerers, bound in shackles; then Indra with his thunderbolt shall cut off their heads!

I, 8. Against sorcerers and demons

1. May this oblation carry hither the sorcerers, as a river (carries) foam! The man or the woman who has performed this (sorcery), that person shall here proclaim himself!

2. This vaunting (sorcerer) has come hither: receive him with alacrity! O Brihaspati, put him into subjection; O Agni and Soma, pierce him through!

3. Slay the offspring of the sorcerer, O soma-drinking (Indra), and subject (him)! Make drop out the farther and the nearer eye of the braggart (demon)!

4. Wherever, O Agni Gâtavedas, thou perceivest the brood of these hidden devourers (atrin), do thou, mightily strengthened by our charm, slay them: slay their (brood), O Agni, piercing them a hundredfold!

I, 16. Charm with lead, against demons and sorcerers

1. Against the devouring demons who, in the night of the full-moon, have arisen in throngs, may Agni, the strong, the slayer of the sorcerers, give us courage!

2. To the lead Varuna gives blessing, to the lead Agni gives help. Indra gave me the lead: unfailingly it dispels sorcery.

3. This (lead) overcomes the vishkandha, this smites the devouring demons (atrin); with this I have overwhelmed all the brood of the Pisâkas.

4. If thou slayest our cow, if our horse or our domestic, we pierce thee with the lead, so that thou shalt not slay our heroes.

VI, 2. The soma-oblation directed against Demons (rakshas)

1. Press the soma, ye priests, and rinse it (for renewed pressing), in behalf of Indra who shall listen to the song of the worshipper, and to my call!

2. Do thou, O doughty (Indra), whom the drops of soma enter as birds a tree, beat off the hostile brood of the Rakshas!

3. Press ye the soma for Indra, the soma-drinker, who wields the thunder-bolt! A youthful victor and ruler is he, praised by many men.

II, 14. Charm against a variety of female demons, conceived as hostile to men, cattle, and home

1. Nissâlâ, the bold, the greedy demon (?dhishana), and (the female demon) with long-drawn howl, the bloodthirsty; all the daughters of Kanda, the Sadânvâs do we destroy.

2. We drive you out of the stable, out of the axle (of the wagon), and the body of the wagon; we chase you, O ye daughters of Magundî, from the house.

3. In yonder house below, there the grudging demons (arâyî) shall exist; there ruin shall prevail, and all the witches!

4. May (Rudra), the lord of beings, and Indra. drive forth from here the Sadânvâs; those that am seated on the foundation of the house Indra shall overcome with his thunderbolt!

5. Whether ye belong to (the demons) of inherited disease, whether ye have been dispatched by men, or whether ye have originated from the Dasyus (demon-like aborigines), vanish from here, O ye Sadânvâs!

6. About their dwelling-places I did swiftly course, as if on a race-course. I have won all contests with you: vanish from here, O ye Sadânvâs!

III, 9. Against vishkandha and kâbava (hostile demons)

1. Of karsapha and visapha heaven is the father and earth the mother. As, ye gods, ye have brought on (the trouble), thus do ye again remove it!

2. Without fastening the), (the protecting plants?) held fast, thus it has been arranged by Manu. The vishkandha do I render impotent, like one who gelds cattle.

3. A talisman tied to a reddish thread the active (seers) then do fasten on: may the fastenings render impotent the eager, fiery kâbava!

4. And since, O ye eager (demons), ye walk like gods by the wile of the Asuras, the fastening (of the amulet) is destructive to the kâbava, as the ape to the dog.

5. I revile thee, the kâbava, unto misfortune, (and) shall work harm for thee. Accompanied with curses ye shall go out like swift chariots!

6. A hundred and one vishkandha are spread out along the earth; for these at the beginning they brought out thee, the amulet, that destroys vish-kandha.

IV, 20. Charm with a certain plant (sadampushpâ) which exposes demons and enemies

1. He sees here, he sees yonder, he sees in the distance, he sees--the sky, the atmosphere as well as the earth, all that, O goddess, he sees.

2. The three heavens, the three earths, and these six directions severally; all creatures may I see through thee, O divine plant!

3. Thou art verily the eyeball of the divine eagle; thou didst ascend the earth as a weary woman a palanquin.

4. The thousand-eyed god shall put this plant into my right hand: with that do I see every one, the Sûdra as well as the Ârya.

5. Reveal (all) forms, do not hide thy own self; moreover, do thou, O thousand-eyed (plant), look the Kimîdins in the face!

6. Reveal to me the wizards, and reveal the witches, reveal all the Pisâkas: for this purpose do I take hold of thee, O plant!

7. Thou art the eye of Kasyapa, and the eye of the four-eyed bitch. Like the sun, moving in the bright day, make thou the Pisâka evident to me!

8. I have dragged out from his retreat the sorcerer and the Kimîdin. Through this (charm) do I see every one, the Sûdra as well as the Ârya.

9. Him that flies in the air, him that moves across the sky, him that regards the earth as his resort, that Pisâka do thou reveal (to me)!

IV, 17. Charm with the apâmârga-plant, against sorcery, demons, and enemies

1. We take hold, O victorious one, of thee, the mistress of remedies. I have made thee a thing of thousandfold strength for ever), one, O plant!

2. Her, the unfailingly victorious one, that wards off curses, that is powerful and defensive; (her and) all the plants have I assembled, intending that she shall save us from this (trouble)!

3. The woman who has cursed us with a curse, who has arranged dire misfortune (for us), who has taken hold of our children, to rob them of their strengthmay she eat (her own) offspring!

4. The magic spell which they have put into the unburned vessel, that which they have put into the blue and red thread, that which they have put into raw flesh, with these slay thou those that have prepared the spell!

5. Evil dreams, troubled life, Rakshas, gruesomeness, and grudging demons (arâyî), all the evil-named, evil-speakinor (powers), these do we drive out from us.

6. Death from hunger, and death from thirst, poverty in cattle, and failure of offspring, all that, O apâmârga, do we wipe out (apa mrigmahe) with thee.

7. Death from thirst, and death from hunger, moreover, ill-luck at dice, all that, O apâmârga, do we wipe out with thee.

8. The apâmârga is sole ruler over all plants, with it do we wipe mishap from thee: do thou then live exempt from disease!

IV, 18. Charm with the apâmârga-plant, against sorcerers and demons

1. Night is like unto the sun, the (starry) night is similar to day. The truth do I engage for help: the enchantments shall be devoid of force!

2. He, O ye gods, who prepares a spell, and carries it to the house of one that knows not (of it), upon him the spell, returning, shall fasten itself like a suckling calf upon its mother!

3. The person that prepares evil at home, and desires with it to harm another, she is consumed by fire, and many stones fall upon her with a loud crash.

4. Bestow curses, O thou (apâmârga), that hast a thousand homes, upon the (demons) visikha ('crestless'), and vigrîva ('crooked-neck')! Turn back the spell upon him that has performed it, as a beloved maid (is brought) to her lover!

5. With this plant I have put to naught all spells, those that they have put into thy field, thy cattle, and into thy domestics.

6. He that has undertaken them has not been able to accomplish them: he broke his foot, his toe. He performed a lucky act for us, but for himself an injury.

7. The apâmârga-plant shall wipe out (apa mârshtu) 'inherited ills, and curses; yea, it shall wipe out all witches, and all grudging demons (arâyî)!

8. Having wiped out all sorcerers, and all grudging demons, with thee, O apâmârga, we wipe all that (evil) out.

IV, 19. Mystic power of the apâmârga-plant, against demons and sorcerers

1. On the one hand thou deprivest of kin, on the other thou now procurest kinfolk. Do thou, moreover, cut the offspring of him that practises spells, as a reed that springs up in the rain!

2. By a Brâhmana thou hast been blest, by Kanva, the descendant of Nrishad. Thou goest like a stronor army; where thou hast arrived, O plant, there there is no fear.

3. Thou goest at the head of the plants, spreading lustre, as if with a light. Thou art on the one hand the protector of the weak, on the other the slayer of the Rakshas.

4. When of yore, in the beginning, the gods drove out the Asuras with thee, then, O plant, thou wast begotten as apâmârga ('wiping out').

5. Thou cuttest to pieces (vibhindatî), and hast a hundred branches; vibhindant ('cutting to pieces') is thy father's name. Do thou (turn) against, and cut to pieces (vi bhindhi) him that is hostile towards us!

6. Non-being arose from the earth, that goes to heaven, (as) a great expansion. Thence, verily, that, spreading vapours, shall turn against the performer (of spells)!

7. Thou didst grow backward, thou hast fruit which is turned backward. Ward off from me all curses, ward off very far destructive weapons!

8. Protect me with a hundredfold, guard me with a thousandfold (strength)! Indra, the strong, shall put strength into thee, O prince of plants!

VII, 65. Charm with the apâmârga-plant, against curses, and the consequences of sinful deeds

1. With fruit turned backward thou verily didst grow, O apâmârga: do thou drive all curses quite far away from here!

2. The evil deeds and foul, or the sinful acts which we have committed, with thee, O apâmârga, whose face is turned to every side, do we wipe them out (apa mrigmahe).

3. If we have sat together with one who has black teeth, or diseased nails, or one who is deformed, with thee, O apâmârga, we wipe all that out (apa mrigmahe).

X, 1. Charm to repel sorceries or spells

1. The (spell) which they skilfully prepare, as a bride for the wedding, the multiform (spell), fashioned by hand, shall go to a distance: we drive it away!

2. The (spell) that has been brought forward by the fashioner of the spell, that is endowed with head, endowed with nose, endowed with ears, and multiform, shall go to a distance: we drive it away!

3. (The spell) that has been prepared by a Sadra, prepared by a Râga, prepared by a woman, prepared by Brahmans, as a wife rejected by her husband, shall recoil upon her fabricator, (and) his kin!

4. With this herb have I destroyed all spells, that which they have put into thy field, into thy cattle, and into thy men.

5. Evil be to him that prepares evil, the curse shall recoil upon him that utters curses: back do we hurl it against him, that it may slay him that fashions the spell.

6. Pratikîna (' Back-hurler'), the descendant of Angiras, is our overseer and officiator (purohita): do thou drive back again (pratîkîh) the spells, and slay yonder fashioners of the spells!

7. He that has said to thee (the spell): 'go on'! upon that enemy, that antagonist do thou turn, O spell: do not seek out us, that are harmless!

8. He that has fitted together thy joints with skill, as the wagoner (Ribhu) the joints of a chariot, to him go, there is thy course: this person here shall remain unknown to thee!

9. They that have prepared thee and taken hold of thee, the cunning wizards-this is what cures it, destroys the spell, drives it back the opposite way - with it do we bathe thee.

10. Since we have come upon the wretched (spell), as upon (a cow) with a dead calf, flooded away (by a river), may all evil go away from me, and mav possessions come to me!

11. If (thy enemies) have made (offerings) to thy Fathers, or have called thy name at the sacrifice, may these herbs free thee from every indigenous evil!

12. From the sin of the gods, and that of the fathers, from mentions of (thy) name, from (evil schemes) concocted at home, may the herbs free thee with might, through (this) charm, (and these) stanzas, (that are) the milk of the Rishis!

13. As the wind stirs up the dust from the earth, and the cloud from the atmosphere, thus may all misfortune, driven by my charm, go away from me!

14. Stride away (O spell), like a loudly braying she-ass, that has been loosened (from the tether); reach those that have fabricated thee, driven from here by (my) forceful charm!

15. 'This is the way, O spell,' with these words do we lead thee. Thee that hast been sent Out against us do we send back again. Go this way like a crushing army, with heavy carts, thou that art multiform, and crowned by a crest(?)!

16. In the distance there is light for thee, hitherward there is no road for thee; away from us take thy course! By another road cross thou ninety navigable streams, hard to cross! Do not injure, go away!

17. As the wind the trees, crush down and fell (the enemy), leave them neither cow, nor horse, nor serving-man! Turn from here upon those that have fabricated thee, O spell, awaken them to childlessness!

18. The spell or the magic which they have buried against thee in the sacrificial straw (barhis), in the field, (or) in the burial-ground, or if with superior skill they have practised sorcery against thee, that art simple and innocent, in thy household fire,--

19. The hostile, insidious instrument which they have brought hither has been discovered; that which has been dug in we have detected. It shall go whence it has been brought hither; there, like a horse, it shall disport itself, and slay the offspring of him that has fashion'ed the spell!

20. Swords of good brass are in our house: we know how many joints thou hast, O spell! Be sure to rise, go away from hence! O stranger, what seekest thou here?

21. I shall hew off, O spell, thy neck, and thy feet: run away! May Indra and Agni, to whom belong the children (of men), protect us!

22. King Soma, who guards and pities us, and the lords of the beings shall take pity on us!
23. May Bhava and Sarva cast the lightning, the divine missile, upon him that performs evil, fashions a spell, and does wrong!

24. If thou art come two-footed, (or) four-footed, prepared by the fashioner of the spell, multiform, do thou, having become eight-footed, again go away from here, O misfortune!

25. Anointed, ornamented, and well equipped, go away, carrying every misfortune! Know, O spell, thy maker, as a daughter her own father!

26. Go away, O spell, do not stand still, track (the enemy) as a wounded (animal)! He is the game, thou the hunter: he is not able to put thee down.

27. Him that first hurls (the arrow), the other, laying on in defence, slays with the arrow, and while the first deals the blow, the other returns the blow.

28. Hear, verily, this speech of mine, and then return whence thou camest, against the one that fashioned thee!

29. Slaughter of an innocent is heinous, O spell: do not slay our cow, horse, or serving-man! Wherever thou hast been put down, thence thee do we remove. Be lighter than a leaf!

30. If ye are enveloped in darkness, covered as if by a net--we tear all spells out from here, send them back again to him that fashioned them.

31. The offspring of them that fashion the spell, practise magic, or plot against us, crush thou, O spell, leave none of them! Slay those that fashion the spell!

32. As the sun is released from darkness, abandons the night, and the streaks of the dawn, thus every misery, (every) device prepared by the fashioner of the spell, (every) misfortune, do I leave behind, as an elephant the dust.

V, 31. Charm to repel sorceries or spells

1. The spell which they have put for thee into an unburned vessel, that which they have put into mixed grain, that which they have put into raw meat, that do I hurl back again.

2. The spell which they have put for thee into a cock, or that which (they have put) into a goat, into a crested animal, that which they have put into a sheep, that do I hurl back again.

3. The spell which they have put for thee into solipeds, into animals with teeth on both sides, that which they have put into an ass, that do I hurl back again.

4. The magic which they have put for thee into moveable property, or into personal possession, the spell which they have put into the field, that do I hurl back again.

5. The spell which evil-scheming persons have put for thee into the gârhapatya-fire, or into the housefire, that which they have put -into the house, that do I hurl back again.

6. The spell which they have put for thee into the assembly-hall, that which (they have put) into the gaming-place, that which they have put into the dice, that do I hurl back again.

7. The spell which they have put for thee into the army, that which they have put into the arrow and the weapon, that which they have put into the drum, that do I hurl back again.

8. The spell which they have placed down for thee in the well, or have buried in the burial-ground, that which they have put into (thy) home, that do I hurl back again.

9. That which they have put for thee into human bones, that which (they have put) into the funeral fire, to the consuming, burning, flesh-eating fire do I hurl that back again.

10. By an unbeaten path he has brought it (the spell) hither, by a (beaten) path we drive it out from here. The fool in his folly has prepared (the spell) aorainst those that are surely wise.

11. He that has undertaken it has not been able to accomplish it: he broke his foot, his toe. He, luckless, performed an auspicious act for us, that are lucky.

12. Him that fashions spells, practises magic, digs after roots, sends out curses, Indra, shall slay with his mighty weapon, Agni shall pierce with his hurled (arrow)!

V, 14. Charm to repel sorceries or spells

1. An eagle found thee out, a boar dug thee out with his snout. Seek thou, O plant, to injure him that seeks to injure (us), strike down him that prepares spells (against us'!

2. Strike down the wizards, strike down him that prepares spells (against us); slay thou, moreover, O plant, him that seeks to injure us!

3. Cutting out from the skin (of the enemy) as if (from the skin) of an antelope, do ye, O gods, fasten the spell upon him that prepares it, as (one fastens) an ornament!

4. Take hold by the hand and lead away the spell back to him that prepares it! Place it in his very presence, so that it shall slay him that prepares the spell!

5. The spells shall take effect upon him that prepares the spells, the curse upon him that pronounces the curse! As a chariot with easy-going wheels, the spell shall turn back upon him that prepares the spell!

6. Whether a woman, or whether a man has prepared the spell for evil, we lead that spell to him as a horse with the halter.

7. Whether thou hast been prepared by the gods, or hast been prepared by men, we lead thee back with the help of Indra as an ally.

8. O Agni gainer of battles, do thou gain the battles! With a counter-charm do we hurl back the spell upon him that prepares the spell.

9. Hold ready, (O plant,) thy weapon, and strike him, slay the very one that has prepared (the spell)! We do not whet thee for the destruction of him that has not practised (spells).

10. Go as a son to his father, bite like an adder that has been stepped upon. Return thou, O spell, to him that prepares the spell, as one who overcomes his fetters!

11. As the shy deer, the antelope, goes out to the mating (buck), thus the spell shall reach him that prepares it!

12. Straighter than an arrow may it (the spell) fly against him, O ye heaven and earth; may that spell take hold again of him that prepares it, as (a hunter)

of his game!

13. Like fire (the spell) shall progress in the teeth of obstacles, like water along its course! As a chariot with easy-going wheels the spell shall turn back upon him that prepares the spell!

VIII, 5. Prayer for protection addressed to a talisman made from wood of the sraktya-tree

1. This attacking talisman, (itself) a man, is fastened upon the man: it is full of force, slays enemies, makes heroes of men, furnishes shelter, provides good luck.

2. This talisman slays enemies, makes strong men, is powerful, lusty, victorious, strong; as a man it advances against sorceries and destroys them.

3. With this talisman Indra slew Vritra, with it he, full of device, destroyed the Asuras, with it he conquered both the heaven and earth, with it he conquered the four regions of space.

4. This talisman of sraktya assails and attacks. With might controlling the enemies, it shall protect us on all sides!

5. Agni has said this, and Soma has said this; Brihaspati, Savitar, Indra (have said) this. These divine purohitas, (chaplains) shall turn back for me (upon the sorcerer) the sorceries with aggressive amulets!

6. I have interposed heaven and earth, also the day, and also the sun. These divine purohitas (chaplains) shall turn back for me (upon the sorcerer) the sorceries with aggressive amulets!

7. (For) the folk that make an armour of the talisman of sraktya--like the sun ascending the sky, it subjects and beats off the sorceries.

8. With the amulet of sraktya, as if with a seer of powerful spirit, I have gained all battles, I slay the enemies, the Rakshas.

9. The sorceries that come from the Angiras, the sorceries that come from the Asuras, the sorceries that prepare themselves, and those that are prepared by others, both these shall go away to a distance across ninety navigable streams!

10. As an armour upon him the gods shall tie the amulet, Indra, Vishnu, Savitar, Rudra, Agni, Pragâpati, Parameshthin, Virâg,Vaisvânara, and the seers all.

11. Thou art the most superb of plants, as if a steer among the cattle, as if a tiger among beasts of prey. (The amulet) that we did seek, that have we found, a guardian at our side.

12. He that wears this talisman, verily is a tiger, a lion as well, and, too, a bull; moreover a curtailer of enemies.

13. Him slay not the Apsaras, nor the Gandharvas, nor mortal men; all reoions does he rule, that wears this talisman.

14. Kasyapa has created thee, Kasyapa has produced thee. Indra wore thee in human (battle); wearing thee in the close combat he conquered. The gods did make the talisman an armour of thousandfold strength.

15. He that plans to harm thee with sorceries, with (unholy) consecrations and sacrifices--him beat thou back, O Indra, with thy thunderbolt that hath a hundred joints!

16. This talisman verily does assail, full of might, victorious. Offspring and wealth it shall protect, provide defence, abound in luck!

17. Remove our enemies in the south, remove our enemies in the north; remove, O Indra, our enemies in the west: light, O hero, place in front (east) of us!

18. An armour for me be heaven and earth, an armour day, an armour the sun! An armour for me be Indra and Agni; Dhâtar shall bestow (dadhAtu) an armour upon me!

19. The armour of Indra and Agni, that is thick and strong, all the gods united do not pierce. This great (armour) shall protect my body on all sides, that I may obtain long life, and reach old age!

20. The divine talisman has ascended upon me,unto completc exemption from injury. Assemble about this post that protects the body, furnishes threefold defence, in order to (secure) strength!

21. Into it Indra shall deposit manliness: do ye, O gods, assemble about it for long life, for life lasting a hundred autumns, that he may reach old age.

22. May Indra who bestows welfare, the lord of the people, the slayer of Vritra, the controller of enemies, he that conquereth and is unconquered, the soma-drinking bull that frees from danger, fasten the amulet upon thee: may it protect thee on each and every side, by day and by night!

X, 3. Praise of the virtues of an amulet derived from the varana-tree

1. Here is my varana-amulet, a bull that destroys the rivals: with it do thou close in upon thy enemies, crush them that desire to injure thee!

2. Break them, crush them, close in upon them: the amulet shall be thy vanguard in front! With the varana the Devas (gods) did ward off (avârayanta) the onslaught of the Asuras (demons) day after day.

3, This thousand-eyed, yellow, golden varanaamulet is a universal cure; it shall lay low thy enemies: be thou the first to injure those that hate thee!

4. This varana will ward off (vârayishyate) the spell that has been spread against thee; this will protect thee from human danger, this will protect thee from all evil!

5. This divine tree, the varana, shall shut out (vârayâtâi)! The gods, too, have shutout (avivaran) the disease that has entered into this (man).

6. If when asleep thou shalt behold an evil dream; as often as a wild beast shall run an inauspicious course; from (ominous) sneezing, and from the evil shriek of a bird, this varana-amulet will protect thee (vârayishyate).

7. From Arâti (grudge), Nirriti (misfortune), from sorcery, and from danger; from death and overstrong weapons the varana will protect thee.

8. The sin that my mother, that my father, that my brothers and my sister have committed; the sin that we (ourselves) have committed, from that this divine tree will protect us.

9. Through the varana are confused my enemies and my (rival) kin. To untraversed gloom they have gone: they shall go to the nethermost darkness!

10. (May) I (be) unharmed, with cows unharmed, long-lived, with undiminished men! This varana-amulet shall guard me in every region (of space)!

11. This varana upon my breast, the kingly, divine tree, shall smite asunder my enemies, as Indra the Dasyus, the Asuras (demons)!

12. Long-lived, a hundred autumns old, do I wear this varana: kingdom and rule, cattle and strength, this shall bestow upon me!

13. As the wind breaks with might the trees, the lords of the forest, thus do thou break my rivals, those formerly born, and the latter born! The varana shall watch over thee!

14. As the wind and the fire consume the trees, the lords of the forest, thus, do thou consume my rivals, those formerly born, and the latter born! The varana shall watch over thee!

15. As, ruined by the wind, the trees lie prostrate, thus do thou ruin and prostrate my rivals, those formerly born, and the latter born! The varana shall watch over thee!

16. Do thou cut off, O varana, before their appointed time and before old age, those that aim to injure him in his cattle, and threaten his sovereignty!

17. As the sun is resplendent, as in him brilliance has been deposited, thus shall the amulet of varana hold fast for me reputation and prosperity, shall sprinkle me with brilliance, and anoint me with splendour!

18. As splendour is in the moon, and in the sun, the beholder of men, thus shall the amulet of varana hold fast, &c.

19. As splendour is in the earth, as in this Gâtavedas (the fire), thus shall the amulet of varana hold fast, &c.

20. As splendour is in the maiden, as in this appointed chariot, thus shall the amulet of varana hold fast, &c.

21. As splendour is in the soma-draught, as splendour is in the honey-mixture (for guests), thus shall the amulet of varana hold fast, &c.

22. As splendour is in the agnihotra-oblation, as splendour is in the call vashat, thus shall the amulet of varana hold fast, &c.

23. As splendour is in the sacrificer, as (splendour) has been deposited in the sacrifice, thus shall the amulet of varana hold fast, &c.

24. As splendour is in Pragâpati, as in this Parameshthin (the lord on high), thus shall the amulet of varana hold fast, &c.

25. As immortality is in the gods, as truth has been deposited in them, thus shall the amulet of varana hod fast, &c.

X, 6. Praise of the virtues of amulet of khadira-wood in the shape of a ploughshare

1. The head of the hostile rival, of the enemy that bates me, do I cut off with might.
2. This amulet, produced by the ploughshare, will prepare an armour for me: full of stirred drink it has come to me, together with sap and lustre.

3. If the skilful workman has injured thee with his hand or with his knife, the living bright waters shall purify thee from that, (so that thou shalt be) bright!

4. This amulet has a golden wreath, bestows faith and sacrifice and might; in our house as a guest it shall dwell!

5. Before it (the amulet as a guest) ghee, surâ (liquor), honey, and every kind of food we place. The amulet having gone to the gods shall, as a father for his sons, plan for us growing good, more and more day after day!

6. The amulet which Brihaspati tied, the ploughshare dripping with ghee, the strong khadira, unto strength, that Agni did fasten on; that yields him ghee more and more day after day: with it those that hate me do thou slay!

7. This amulet which Brihaspati tied that Indra did fasten on, for strength and heroism; that yields him might more and more, &c.

8. The amulet which Brihaspati tied . . . that Soma did fasten on unto perfect hearing and seeing; that verily yields him lustre more and more, &c.

9. The amulet which Brihaspat, tied . . . that Sûrya did fasten on, with that he conquered these directions of space; that yields him prosperity moreand more, &c.

10. The amulet which Brihaspati tied wearing that amulet Kandramas (the moon) conquered the golden cities of the Asuras and the Dânavas; that yields him fortune more and more, &c.

11. The amulet which Brihaspat' tied for swift Vâta (wind), that yields him strength more and more, &c.
12, The amulet which Brihaspati tied for swift Vâta, with that amulet, O Asvins, do ye guard this plough-land; that yields the two physicians (the Asvins) might more and more, &c.

13. The amulet which Brihaspati tied for swift Vâta, wearing that, Savitar through it conquered this light; that yields him abundance more and more, &c.

14. The amulet which Brihaspati tied for swift Vâta, wearing that, the waters ever run undiminished; that verily yields them ambrosia more and more, &c.

15. The amulet which Brihaspati tied for swift Vâta, that comforting amulet king Varuna did fasten on; that verily yields him truth more and more, &c.

16. The amulet which Brihaspati tied for swift Vâta, wearing that the gods did conquer all the worlds in battle; that verily yields them conquest more and more, &c.

17. The amulet which Brihaspati tied for swift Vâta, that comforting amulet the divinities did fasten on; that verily yields them- all more and more, &c.

18. The seasons did fasten it on; the divisions (of the year) did fasten it on. Since the year did fasten it on, it guards every being.

19. The intermediate directions did fasten it on; the directions did fasten it on. The amulet created by Pragâpati has subjected those that hate me.

20. The Atharvans did tie it on, the descendants of the Atharvans did tie it on; with these allied, the Angiras cleft the castles of the Dasyus. With it those that hate me do thou slay!

21. That Dhâtar did fasten on: (then) he shaped the being. With it those that hate me do thou slay!
22. The amulet which Brihaspati tied for the gods, destructive of the Asuras, that has come to me together with sap and lustre.

23. The amulet . . . has come to me together with cows, goats, and sheep, together with food and offspring.

24. The amulet . . . has come to me together with rice and barley, together with might and prosperity.

25. The amulet has come to me with a stream of honey and ghee together with sweet drink.

26. The amulet has come to me together with nourishment and milk, together with goods and fortune.

27. The amulet . . . has. come to me together with brilliance and strength, together with glory and reputation.

28. The amulet . . . has come to me together with all 'kinds of prosperity.

29, This amulet the gods shall give me unto prosperity, the mighty amulet that strengthens sovereignty and injures the rivals!

30. An (amulet) auspicious for me thou shalt fasten upon (me), together with brahma (spiritual exaltation) and brilliance! Free from rivals, slaying rivals, it has subjected my rivals.

31. This god-born amulet, the sap milked from which these three worlds revere, shall render me superior to him that hates me; it shall ascend upon my head unto excellence!

32. The amulet upon which the gods, the Fathers, and men ever live, shall ascend upon my head unto excellence!

33. As the seed grows in the field, in the furrow drawn by the ploughshare, thus in me offspring, cattle, and every kind of food shall grow up!

34. Upon whom, O thou amulet that prosperest the sacrifice, I have fastened thee (that art) propitious, him, O amulet, that yieldest a hundred-fold sacrificial reward, thou shalt inspire unto excellence!

35. This fire-wood that has been laid on together with the oblations do thou, Agni, gladly accept: may we in this kindled Gâtavedas (fire), through (this) charm, find favour, well-being, offspring, sight, and cattle!

IV, 16. Prayer to Varuna for protection against treacherous designs

1. The great guardian among these (gods) sees as if from anear. He that thinketh he is moving stealthily--all this the gods know.

2. If a man stands, walks, or sneaks about, if he goes slinking away, if he goes into his hiding-place; if two persons sit together and scheme, king Varuna is there as a third, and knows it.

3. Both this earth here belongs to king Varuna, and also yonder broad sky whose boundaries are far away. Moreover these two oceans are the loins of Varuna; yea, he is hidden in this small (drop of) water.

4. He that should flee beyond the heaven far away would not be free from king Varuna. His spies come hither (to the earth) from heaven, with a thousand eyes do they watch over the earth.

5. King Varuna sees through all that is between heaven and earth, and all that is beyond. He has counted the winkings of men's eyes. As a (winning) gamester puts down his dice, thus does he establish these (laws).

6. May all thy fateful toils which, seven by seven, threefold, lie spread out, ensnare him that speaks falsehood: him that speaks the truth they shall let go!

7. With a hundred snares, O Varuna, surround him, let the liar not go free from thee, O thou that observest men! The rogue shall sit, his belly hanging loose, like a cask without hoops, bursting all about!

8. With (the snare of) Varuna which is fastened lengthwise, and that which (is fastened) broadwise, with the indigenous and the foreign, with the divine and the human,--

9. With all these snares do I fetter thee, O N. N., descended from N. N., the son of the woman N. N.: all these do I design for thee.

II, 12. Imprecation against enemies thwarting holy work

1. Heaven and earth, the broad atmosphere, the goddess of the field, and the wonderful, far-striding (Vishnu); moreover, the broad atmosphere guarded by Vâta (the wind): may these here be inflamed, when I am inflamed!

2. Hear this, O ye revered gods! Let Bharadvâga recite for me songs of praise! 'May he who injures this our plan be bound in the fetter (of disease) and joined to misfortune!

3. Hear, O soma-drinking Indra, what with burning heart I shout to thee! I cleave, as one cleaves a tree with an axe, him that injures this our plan.

4. With (the aid of) thrice eighty siman-singers, with (the aid of) the Âdityas, Vasus, and Angiras--may our father's sacrifices and gifts to the priests, aid us-do I seize this one with fateful fervour.

5. May heaven and earth look after me, may all the gods support me! O ye Angiras, O ye fathers devoted to Soma, may he who does harm enter into misfortune!

6 . He who perchance despises us, O ye Maruts, he who abuses the holy practice which is beiog performed by us, may his evil deeds be firebrands to him, may the heavens surround with fire the hater of holy practices!

7. Thy seven in-breathings and thy eight marrows, these do I cut for thee by means of my charm. Thou shalt go to the seat of Yama, fitly prepared, with Agni as thy guide!

8. I set thy footstep upon the kindled fire. May Agni surround thy body, may thy voice enter into breath!

VII, 70. Frustration of the sacrifice of an enemy

1. Whenever yonder person in his thought, and with his speech, offers sacrifice accompanied by oblations and benedictions, may Nirriti (the goddess of destruction), allying herself with death, smite his offering before it takes effect!

2. May sorcerers, Nirriti, as well as Rakshas, mar his true work with error! May the gods, despatched by Indra, scatter (churn) his sacrificial butter; may that which yonder person offers not succeed!

3. The two agile supreme rulers, like two eagle-s pouiicing down, shall strike the sacrificial butter pf the enemy, whosoever plans evil against us!

4. Back do I tie both thy two arms, thy mouth I shut. With the fury of god Agni, have I destroyed thy oblation.

5. I tie thy two arms, I shut thy mouth. With the fury of terrible Agni have I destroyed thy oblation.

II, 7. Charm against curses and hostile plots, undertaken with a certain plant

1. The god-begotten plant, hated by the wicked, which wipes away the curses (of the enemies), like water a foul spot it has washed away all curses from me.

2. The curse of the rival and the curse of the kinswoman, the curse which the Brahman shall utter in wrath, all that (do thou put) under our feet!

3. From heaven her root is suspended, from the earth it rises up; with her that has a thousand shoots do thou protect us on all sides!

4. Protect me, protect my offspring, protect our goods; let not ill-will overcome us, let not hostile schemes overcome us!

5. The curse shall go to the curser; joint possession shall we have with the friend. Of the enemy who bewitches with (his) eye we hew off the ribs.

III, 6. The asvattha-tree as a destroyer of enemies

1. A male has sprung from a male, the asvattha (ficus religiosa) from the khadira (acacia catechu). May this slay my enemies, those whom I hate and those who hate me!

2. Crush the enemies, as they rush on, O asvattha, 'displacer,' allied with Indra, the slayer of Vritra, (allied) with Mitra and Varuxa!

3. As thou didst break forth, O asvattha, into the great flood (of the air), thus do thou break up all those whom I hate and those who hate me!

4. Thou that goest conquering as a conquering bull, with thee here, O asvattha, may we conquer our rivals!

5. May Nirriti (the goddess of destruction), O asvattha, bind in the toils of death that cannot be loosened those enemies of mine whom I hate and who hate me!

6. As thou climbest up the trees, O asvattha, and renderest them subordinate, thus do thou split in two the head of iny enemy, and overcome him!

7. They (the enemies) shall float down like a ship cut loose from its moorings! There is no returning again for those that have been driven out by the 'displacer.'

8. I drive them out with my mind, drive them out with my thought, and also with my incantation. We drive them out with a branch of the asvattha-tree.

VI, 75. Oblation for the suppression of enemies (nairbâdhyam havih)

1. Forth from his home do I drive that person yonder, who as a rival contends with us: through the oblation devoted to suppression Indra, has broken him to pieces.

2. Indra, the slayer of Vritra, shall drive him to the remotest distance, from which in all successive years he shall not again return!

3. He shall go to the three distances, he shall go beyond the five peoples; he shall go beyond the three ethers, whence he shall not again in all successive years return, while the sun is upon the heavens!

VII 37. Curse against one that practises hostile charms

1. The thousand-eyed curse having yoked his chariot has come hither, seeking out him that curses me, as a wolf the house of him that owns sheep.

2. Avoid us, O curse, as a burning fire (avoids) a lake! Strike here him that curses us, as the lightning of heaven the tree!

3. He that shall curse us when we do not curse, and he that shall curse us when we do curse, him do I hurl to death as a bone to a dog upon the ground.

VII, 13. Charm to deprive enemies of their strength

1. As the rising sun takes away the lustre of the stars, thus do I take away the strength of both the women and the men that hate me.

2. As many enemies as ye are, lookina out auainst me, as I come on--of those that hate me do I take away the strenorth, as the sun takes away the strength of persons asleep (while it rises).

CHARMS PERTAINING TO WOMEN (STRIKARATÂNI)

II, 36. Charm to obtain a husband

1. May, O Agni, a suitor after our own heart come to us, may he come to this maiden with our fortune! May she, agreeable to suitors, charming at festivals, promptly obtain happiness through a husband!

2. Agreeable to Soma, agreeable to Brahma, arranged by Aryaman, with the unfailing certainty of god Dhâtar, do I bestow upon thee good fortune, the acquisition of a husband.

3. This woman shall obtain a hnsband, since king Soma makes her lovely! May she, begetting sons, become a queen; may she, going to her husband, shine in loveliness!

4. As this comfortable cave, O Maghavan (Indra), furnishing a safe abode, hath become pleasing to animals, thus may this woman be a favourite of fortune (Bhaga), beloved, not at odds with her husband!

5. Do thou ascend the full, inexhaustible ship of Bhaga (fortune); upon this bring, hither the suitor who shall be agreeable (to thee)!

6. Bring hither by thy shouts, O lord of wealth, the suitor, bend his mind towards her; turn thou the right side of every agreeable suitor towards (her)!

7. This gold and bdellium, this balsam, and Bhaga (fortune), too; these have prepared thee for husbands, that thou mayest obtain the one that is agreeable.

8. Hither to thee Savitar shall lead the husband that is agreeable! Do thou, O herb, bestow (him) upon her!

VI, 60. Charm for obtaining a husband

1. This Aryaman (wooer) with loosened crest of hair comes hither in front (of the procession), seeking a husband for this spinster, and a wife for this wifeless man.

2. This maid, O Aryaman, has wearied of going to the wedding-feasts of other women. Now shall, without fail, O Aryaman, other women go to her wedding-feast!

3. Dhâtar (the creator) supports (didhhra) this earth, Dhâtar supports the heavens, and the sun. May Dhatar furnish this spinster with a husband after her own heart).

VI, 82. Charm for obtaining a wife

1. I call the name of him that comes here, that hath come here, and is arriving; I crave (the name) of Indra, Vritra's slayer, the Visava, of hundred-fold strength.

2. The road by which the Asvins carried away as a bride Sûryâ, Savitar's daughter,'by that road,' Bhaga (fortune) told me, 'thou shalt bring here a wife'!

With thy wealth-procuring, great, golden hook, O Indra, husband of Sakî, procure a wife for me that desireth a wife!

VI, 78. Blessing for a married couple

1. Through this oblation, that causes prosperity, may this man flourish anew; may he excel the wife that they have brought to him with his sap!

2. May he excel in strength, excel in royalty! May this couple be inexhaustible in wealth that bestows thousandfold lustre!

3. Tvashtar begot (for thee) a wife, Tvashtar for her begot thee as a husband. May Tvashtar bestow upon you two a thousand lives, may he bestow upon you long life!

VII, 36. Love-charm spoken by a bridal couple

1. The eyes of us two shine like honey, our foreheads gleam like ointment. Place me within thy heart; may one mind be in common to us both!

VII, 37. Charm pronounced by the bride over the bridegroom

1. I envelope thee in my garment that was produced by Manu (the first man), that thou shalt be mine alone, shalt not even discourse of other women!

VI, 81. A bracelet as an amulet to ensure conception

1. A holder art thou, holdest both hands, drivest off the Rakshas. An acquirer of offspring and wealth this bracelet hath become!

2. O bracelet, open up the womb, that the embryo be put (into it)! Do thou, O limit (-setting bracelet), furnish a son, bring him here (A gamaya), thou that comest here (Agame)!

3. The bracelet that Aditi wore, when she desired a son.Tvashtar shall fasten upon this woman, intending that she shall beget a son.

III, 23. Charm for obtaining a son (pumsavanam)

1. That which has caused thee to miscarry do we drive away from thee, that very thing do we deposit outside of thee, away in a far place.

2. Into thy womb shall enter a male germ, as an arrow into a quiver! May a man be born there, a son ten months old!

3. A male son do thou produce, and after him a male shall be born! Thou shalt be the mother of sons, of those who are born, and those whom thou shalt bear!

4. By the effective seed which bulls put forth do thou obtain a son; be a fruitful milch-cow!

5. Pragâpati's (the lord of creatures) work do I perform for thee: may the germ enter into thy womb! Obtain thou, woman, a son who shall bring prosperity to thee, and bring thou pi-osperity to him!

6. The plants whose father was the sky, whose mother the earth, Whose root the (heavenly) ocean--may those divine herbs aid thee in obtaining a son!

VI, 11. Charm for obtaining a son (pumsavanam)

1. The asvattha (ficus religiosa) has mounted the samî (mimosa suma): then a male child was produced. That, forsooth, is the way to obtain a son; that do we bring to (our) wives.

2. In the male, forsooth, seed doth grow, that is poured into the female. That, forsooth, is the way to obtain a son; that has been told by Pragâpati.

3. Pragâpati, Anumati, and Sinîvâlî have fashioned him. May he (Pragâpati) elsewhere afford the birth of a female, but here he shall bestow a man!

VII, 35. An incantation to make a woman sterile

1. The other enemies conquer with might; beat back, O Gâtavedas, those that are not yet born! Enrich this kingdom unto happiness, may all the gods acclaim this man!

2. Of these hundred entrails of thine, as well as of the thousand canals, of all these have I closed the openings with a stone.

3. The upper part of the womb do I place below, there shall come to thee neither offspring nor birth! I render thee sterile and devoid of offspring; a stone do I make into a cover for thee.

VI, 17. Charm to prevent miscarriage

1. As this great earth conceives the germs of the beings, thus shalt thy embryo be-beld fast, to produce a child after pregnancy!

2. As this great earth holds these trees, thus shall thy embryo be held fast, to produce a child after pregnancy!

3. As this great earth holds the mountains and the peaks, thus shall thy embryo be held fast, to produce a child after pregnancy!

4. As this great earth holds the animals scattered far, thus shall thy embryo be held fast, to produce a child after pregnancy!

I, 11. Charm for easy parturition

1. Aryaman as active hotar-priest shall utter for thee the vashat-call at this (soma-) pressing, O Pûshan! May (this) woman, (herself) begotten in

the proper way, be delivered, may her joints relax, that she shall bring forth!

2. Four directions has the heaven, and also four the earth: (from these) the gods created the embryo. May they open her, that she shall bring forth!

3. May Sûshan open: her womb do we cause to gape. Do thou, O Sûshan, loosen the womb, do thou, O Bishkalâ, let go (the ernbryo)!

4. Attached not at all to the flesh, nor to the fat, not at all to the marrow, may the splotched, moist, placenta come down to be eaten by a dog! May the placenta fall down!

5. I split open thy vagina, thy womb, thy canals; I separate the mother and the son, the child along with the placenta. May the placenta fall down!

6. As flies the wind, as flies the mind, as fly the winged birds, so do thou, O embryo,. ten months old, fall along with the placenta! May the placenta fall down!

I, 34. Charm with licorice, to secure the love of a woman

1. This plant is born of honey, with honey do we dig for thee. Of honey thou art begotten, do thou make us full of honey!

2. At the tip of my tongue may I have honey, at my tongue's root the sweetness of honey! In my power alone shalt thou then be, thou shalt come up to my wish!

3. Sweet as honey is my entrance, sweet as honey my departure. With my voice do I speak sweet as honey, may I become like honey!

4. I am sweeter than honey, fuller of sweetness than licorice. Mayest thou, without fail, long for me alone, (as a bee) for a branch full of honey!

5. I have surrounded thee with a clinging sugarcane, to remove aversion, so that thou shalt not be averse to me!

II, 30. Charm to secure the love of a woman

1. As the wind tears this grass from the surface of the earth, thus do I tear thy soul, so that thou, woman, shalt love, shalt not be averse to me!

2. If ye, O two Asvins, shall unite and bring together the loving pair-united are the fortunes of,both of you (lovers), united the thoughts, united the purposes!

3. When birds desire to chirp, lustily desire to chirp, may my call go there, as an arrow-point upon the shaft!

4. What is within shall be without, what is without shall be within! Take captive, O herb, the, soul of the maidens endowed with every chai-m!

5. Longing for a husband this woman hath come, I have come longing for a wife, As a loudly neighing horFe I have attained to my good fortune!

VI, 8. Charm to secure the love of a woman

1. As the creeper embraces the tree on all sides, thus do thou embrace me, so that thou, woman, shalt love me, so that thou shalt not be averse to me!

2. As the eagle when he flies forth presses his wings against the earth, thus do I fasten down thy mind, so that thou, woman, shalt love me, so that thou shalt not be averse to me.

3. As the sun day by day goes about this heaven and earth, thus do I go about thy mind, so that thou, woman, shalt love me, so that thou shalt not be: averse to me.

VI, 9. Charm to secure the love of a woman

1. Hanker thou after my body, my feet, hanker after my eyes, my thighs! The eyes of thee, as thou lustest after me, and thy hair shall be parched with love?

2. I make thee cling to my arm, cling to my heart, so that thou shalt be in my power, shalt come up to my wish!

3. The cows, the mothers of the ghee, who lick their young, in whose heart love is planted, shall make yonder woman bestow love upon me!

VI, 102. Charm to secure the love of a woman

1. As this draught animal, O ye Asvins, comes on, and proceeds, thus may thy soul come on, and proceed to me!

2. I draw to myself thy mind, as the leading stallion the female side-horse. As the stalk of grass torn by the wind, thus shall thy mind fasten itself upon me!

3. A coaxing mixture of salve, of sweet wood, of kushtha, and of spikenard, do I deftly pick out with the hands of Bhaga (good fortune).

III, 25. Charm to arouse the passionate love of a woman

1. May (love), the disquieter, disquiet thee; do not hold out upon thy bed! With the terrible arrow of Kâma (love) do I pierce thee in the heart.

2. The arrow, winged with longing, barbed with love, whose shaft is undeviating desire, with that, well-aimed, Kâma shall pierce thee in the heart!

3. With that well-aimed arrow of Kâma which parches the spleen, whose plume flies forward, which burns up, do I pierce thee in the heart.

4. Consumed by burning ardour, with parched mouth, do thou (woman) come to me, pliant, (thy) pride laid aside, mine alone, speaking sweetly and to me devoted!

5. I drive thee with a goad from thy mother and thy father, so that thou shalt be in my power, shalt come up to my wish.

6. All her thoughts do ye, O Mitra and Varuna, drive out of her! Then, having deprived her of her will,.put her into my power alone!

VII, 139. Charm to arouse the passionate love of a woman

1. Clinging to the ground thou didst grow, (O plant), that producest bliss for me; a hundred branches extend from thee, three and thirty grow down from thee: with this plant of a thousand leaves thy heart do I parch.

2. Thy heart shall parch (with love) for me, and thy mouth shall parch (with love for me)! Languish, moreover, with love for me, with parched mouth pass thy days!

3. Thou that causest affection, kindlest (love), brown, lovely (plant), draw (us) together; draw together yonder woman and myself, our hearts make the same!

4. As the mouth of him that hath not drunk dries tip, thus languish thou with love for me, with parched mouth pass thy days!

5. As the Ichneumon tears the serpent, and joins him together again, thus, O potent (plant), join together what hath been torn by love!

VII, 38. Charm to secure the love of a man

1. This potent herb do I dig out: it draws toward me the eve, causes (love's) tears. It brings back him who has gone to a distance, rejoices him that approaches me.

2. By (the plant) with which the Âsurî allured Indra away from the gods, by that do I subject thee, that I may be well-beloved of thee!

3. Thy face is turned towards Soma (the nioon), thy face is turned towards Sûrya (the sun), thy face is turned towards all the gods: 't is tliee here that we do invoke.

4. My speech, not thine, (in this matter) hath weight: in the assembly, forsooth, do thou speak! To me alone shalt thou belong, shalt not even discourse of other women!

5. Whether thou art beyond the haunts of men, or whether across the river, this very herb, as if a captive bound, shall bring, thee back to me!

VI, 130. Charm to arouse the passionate love of a man

1. This yearning love comes from the Apsaras, the victorious, imbued with victory. Ye gods, send forth the yearning love: may yonder man burn after me!

2. My wish is, he shall long for me, devoted he shall long for me! Ye gods, send forth the yearning love: may yonder man burn after me!

3. That yonder man shall long for me, (but) I for him nevermore, ye gods, send forth the yearning love: may yonder man burn after me!

4. Do ye, O Maruts, intoxicate him (With love); do thou, O mid-air, intoxicate him; do thou, O Agni, intoxicate him! May yonder man burn after me!

VI, 131. Charm to arouse the passionate love of a man

1. From thy head unto thy feet do I implant (love's) longing into thee. Ye gods, send forth the yearning love: may yonder man burn after me!

2. Favour this (plan), Anumati; fit it tooether, Âkûti! Ye gods, send forth the yearning love may yonder man burn after me!

3. If thou dost run three leagues away, (or even) five leagues, the distance coursed by a horseman, from there thou shalt again return, shalt be the father of our sons!

VI, 132. Charm to arouse the passionate love of a man

1. Love's consuming longing, together with yearning, which the gods have poured into the waters, that do I kindle for thee by the law of Varuna!

2. Love's consuming longing, together with yearning, which the all-gods (visve devâh) have poured into the waters, that do I kindle for thee by the law of Varuna!

3. Love's consuming longing, together with yearning, which Indrâni has poured into the waters, that do I kindle for thee by the law of Varuna!

4. Love's consuming longing, together with yearning, which Indra and Agni have poured into the waters, that do I kindle for thee by the law of Varuna!

5. Love's consuming longing, together with yearning, which Mitra and Varuna have poured into the waters, that do I kindle for thee by the law of Varuna!

IV, 5. Charm at an assignation

1. The bull with a thousand horns who rose out of the sea, with the aid of him, the mighty one, do we put the folks to sleep.

2. The wind blows not over the earth. No one looks on. Do thou then, befriended of Indra, put all women and dogs to sleep!

3. The women that lie upon couches and upon beds, and they that rest in litters, the women all that exhale sweet fragrance, do we put to sleep.

4. Every moving thing I have held fast. Eye and breath I have held fast. I have held fast all limbs in the deep gloom of the night.

5. Of him that sits, and him that walks, of him that stands and looks about, of these the eyes we do shut, just as these premises (are shut).

6. The mother shall sleep, the father shall sleep, the dog shall sleep, the lord of the house shall sleep! All her relations shall sleep, and these people round about shall sleep!

7. O sleep, put thou to sleep all people with the magic that induces sleep! Put the others to sleep until the sun rises; may I be awake until the dawn appears, like Indra, unharmed, uninjured!

VI, 77. Charm to cause the return of a truant woman

1. The heavens have stood, the earth has stood, all creatures have stood. The mountains have stood upon their foundation, the horses in the stable I have caused to stand.

2. Him that has control of departure, that has control of coming home, return, and turning in, that shepherd do I also call.

3. O Gâtavedas (Agni), cause thou to turn ill; a hundred way's hither shall be thine, a thousand modes of return shall be thine: with these do thou restore us again!

VI, 18. Charm to allay jealousy

1. The first impulse of jealousy, moreover the one that comes after the first, the fire, the heart-burning, that do wc waft away from thee.

2. As the earth is dead in spirit, in spirit more dead than the dead, and as the spirit of him that has died, thus shall the spirit of the jealous (man) be dead!

3. Yon fluttering little spirit that has been fixed into thy heart, from it the jealousy do I remove, as air from a water-skin.

VII, 45. Charm to allay jealousy

1. From folk belonging to all kinds of people, from the Sindhu (Indus) thou hast been brought hither: from a distance, I ween, has been fetched the very remedy for jealousy.

2. As if a fire is burning him, as if the forest-fire burns in various directions, this jealousy of his do thou quench, as a fire (is quenched) with water!

I, 14. A woman's incantation against her rival

1. I have taken unto myself her fortune and her glory, as a wreath off a tree. Like a mountain with broad foundation may she sit a long time with her parents!

2. This woman shall be subjected to thee as thy wife, O king Yama; (till then) let her be fixed to the house of her mother, or her brother, or her father!

3. This woman shall be the keeper of thy house, O king (Yama), and her do we make over to thee! May she long sit with her relatives, until (her hair) drops from her head!

4. With the incantation of Asita, of Kasyapa, and of Gaya do I cover up thy fortune, as women cover (something) within a chest.

III, 18. Charm of a woman against a rival or co-wife

1. I dig up this plant, of herbs the most potent, by whose power rival women are overcome, and husbands are obtained.

2. O thou (plant) with erect leaves, lovely, do thou, urged on by the gods, full of might, drive away my rival, make my h usband mine alone!

3. He did not, forsooth, call thy name, and thou shalt not delight in this' husband! To the very farthest distance do we drive our rival.

4. Superior am I, O superior (plant), superior, truly, to superior (women). Now shall my rival be inferior to those that are inferior!

5. I am overpowering, and thou, (O plant), art completely overpowering. Having both grown full of power, let us overpower my rival!

6. About thee (my husband) I have placed the overpowering (plant), upon thee placed the very overpowering one. May thy mind run after me as a calf after the cow, as water along its course!

VI, 138. Charm for depriving a man of his virility

1. As the best of the plants thou art reputed, O herb: turn this man for me to-day into a eunuch that wears his hair dressed!

2. Turn him into a eunuch that wears his hair dressed, and into one that wears a hood! Then Indra with a pair of stones shall break his testicles both!

3. O eunuch, into a eunuch thee I have turned;O castrate, into a castrate thee I have turned; O weakling, into a weakling thee I have turned! A hood upon his head, and a hair-net do we place.

4. The two canals, fashioned by the gods, in which man's power rests, in thy testicles . . . . I break them with a club.

5. As women break reeds for a mattress with a stone, thus do I break thy member.

I, 18. Charm to remove evil bodily characteristics from a woman

1. The (foul) mark, the lalâmî (with spot on the forehead), the Arâti (grudging demon), do we drive out. Then the (signs) that are auspicious (shall remain) with us; (yet) to beget offspring do we bring the Arâti!

2. May Savitar drive out uncouthness from her feet, may Varuna, Mitra, and Aryaman (drive it) out from her hands; may Anumati kindly drive it out for us! For happiness the gods have created this woman.

3. The fierceness that is in thyself, in thy body, or in thy look, all that do we strike away with our charm. May god Savitar prosper thee!

4. The goat-footed, the bull-toothed, her who scares the cattle, the snorting one, the vilîdhî (the driveling one), the lalâmî (with spot on the forehead), these do we drive from us.

VI, 110. Expiatory charm for a child born under an unlucky star

1. Of yore, (O Agni), thou wast worthy of supplication at the sacrifice; thou wast the priest in olden times, and now anew shalt sit (at our sacrifice)! Delight, O Agni, thy own body, and, sacrificing, bring good fortune here to us!

2. Him that hath been born under the (constellation) gyeshihaghnî ('she that slays the oldest'), or under the vikritâu ('they that uproot'), save thou from being torn up by the root by Yama (death)! May be (Agni) guide him across all misfortunes to long life, to a life of a hundred autumns!

3. On a tiger (-like) day the hero was born; born under a (good) constellation he becometh a mighty hero. Let him not slay, when he grows up, his father, let him not injure the mother that hath begotten him!

VI, 140. Expiation for the irregular appearance of the first pair of teeth

1. Those two teeth, the tigers, that have broken forth, eager to devour father and mother, do thou, O Brahmanaspati Gâtavedas, render auspicious!

2. Do ye eat rice, eat barley, and eat, too, beans, as well as sesamum! That, O teeth.. is the share deposited for your enrichment. Do not injure father and mother!

3. Since ye have been invoked, O teeth, be ye in unison kind and propitious! Elsewhere, O teeth, shall pass away the fierce (qualities) of your body! Do not injure father and mother!

CHARMS PERTAINING TO ROYALTY (RÂGA-KARMÂNI)

IV, 8. Prayer at the consecration of a king

1. Himself prosperous (bhûto), he does put strength into the beings (bhûteshu); he became the chief lord of the beings (bhûtânâm). To his consecration death does come: may he, the king, favour this kingdom!

2. Come forth hither-do not glance away-as a mighty guardian, slayer of enemies! Step hither, thou who prosperest thy friends: the gods shall bless thee!

3. As he did step hither all (men) did attend him. Clothed in grace, he moves, shining by his own lustre. This is the great name of the manly Asura; endowed with every form (quality) he entered upon immortal (deeds).

4. Thyself a tiger, do thou upon this tiger-skin stride (victorious) through the great regionst All the clans shall wish for thee, and the heavenly waters, rich in sap!

5. The heavenly waters, rich in sap, flow joyously, (and too) those in the sky and upon the earth: with the lustre of all of these do I sprinkle thee.

6. They have sprinkled thee with their lustre., the heavenly waters rich in sap. May Savitar thus fashion thee, that thou shalt prosper thy friends!

7. (The waters) thus embracing him, the tiger, promote him, the lion, to great good fortune. Him, the leopard in the midst of the waters, as though standing in the ocean, the beneficent (floods, or the vigorous priests) cleanse thoroughly!

III, 3. Charm for the restoration of an exiled king

1. (Agni) has shouted loud: may he here well perform his work! Spread thyself out, O Agni, over the far-reaching hemispheres of the world! The

all-possessing Maruts shall engage thee: bring hither that (king) who devoutly spends the offering!

2. However far he be, the red (steeds) shall urge hither Indra, the seer, to friendship, since the gods, (chanting) for him the gâyatri, the brihatî, and the arka (songs), infused courage into him with the sautrâmanî-sacrifice!

3. From the waters king Varuna shall call thee, Soma shall call thee from the mountains, Indra shall cite thee to these clans! Turn into an eagle and fly to these clans!

4. An eagle shall bring hither from a distance him that is fit to be called, (yet) wanders exiled in a strange land! The Asvins shall prepare for thee a path, easy to travel! Do ye, his kinfolk, gather close about him!

5. Thy opponents shall call thee; thy friends have chosen. thee! Indra, Agni, and all the gods have kept prosperity with this people.

6. The kinsman or the stranger that opposes thy call, him, O Indra, drive away; then render this (king) accepted here!

III, 4. Prayer at the election of a king

1. (Thy) kingdom hath come to thee: arise, endowed with lustre! Go forth as the lord of the people, rule (shine) thou, a universal ruler! All the regions of the compass shall call thee, O king; attended and revered be thou here!

2. Thee the clans, thee these regions, goddesses five, shall choose for empire! Root thyself upon the height, the pinnacle of royalty: then do thou, mighty, distribute goods among us!

3. Thy kinsmen with calls shall come to thee; agile Agni shall go with them as messenger! Thy wives, thy sons shall be devoted to thee; being a mighty (ruler) thou shalt behold rich tribute!

4. The Asvins first, Mitra and Varuna both, all the gods, and the Maruts, shall call thee! Then fix thy mind upon the bestowal of wealth, then do thou, mighty, distribute wealth among us!

5. Hither hasten forth from the farthest distance heaven and earth, both, shall be propitious to thee! Thus did this king Varuna (as if, 'the chooser') decree that; he himself did call thee: 'come thou hither'!

6. O Indra, Indra, come thou to the tribes of men, for thou hast agreed, concordant with the Varunas (as if,'the electors'), He did call thee to thy own domain (thinking): 'let him revere the gods, and manage, too, the people'!

7. The rich divinities of the roads, of manifold diverse forms, all coming together have given thee a broad domain. They shall all concordantly call thee; rule here, a mighty, benevolent (king), to up the tenth decade (of thy life)!

III, 5. Praise of an amulet derived from the parna-tree, designed to strengthen royal power

1. Hither hath come this amulet of parna-wood, with its might mightily crushing the enemy. (It is) the strength of the gods, the sap of the waters: may it assiduously enliven me with energy!

2. The power to rule thou shalt hold fast in me, O amulet of parna-wood; wealth (thou shalt hold fast) in me! May I, rooted in the domain of royalty, become the chief!

3. Their very own amulet which the gods deposited secretly in the tree, that the gods shall give us to wear, together with life!

4. The parna has come hither as the mighty strength of the soma, given by Indra, instructed by Varuna. May I, shining brilliantly, wear it, unto long life, during a hundred autumns!

5. The amulet of parna-wood has ascended upon me unto complete exemption from injury, that I may rise superior (even) to friends and alliances!

6. The skilful builders of chariots, and the ingenious workers of metal, the folk about me all, do thou, O parna, make my aids!

7. The kings who (themselves) make kings, the charioteers, and leaders of hosts, the folk about me all, do thou, O parna, make my aids!

8. Thou art the body-protecting parna, a 'liero, brother of me, the hero. Along with the brilliancy of the year do I fasten thee on, O amulet!

IV, 22. Charm to secure the superiority of a king

1. This warrior, O Indra, do thou strengthen for me, do thou install this one as sole ruler (bull) of the Vis (the people); emasculate all his enemies, subject them to him in (their) contests!

2. To him apportion his share of villages, horses, and cattle; deprive of his share the one that is his enemy! May this king be the pinnacle of royalty; subject to him, O Indra, every enemy!

3. May this one be the treasure-lord of riches, may this king be the tribal lord of the Vis (the people)! Upon this one, O Indra, bestow great lustre, devoid of lustre render his enemy!

4. For him shall ye, O heaven and earth, milk ample good, as two milch-cows yielding warm milk! May this king be favoured of Indra, favoured of cows, of plants, and cattle!

5. I unite with thee Indra who has supremacy, through whom one conquers and is not (himself) conquered, who shall install thee as sole ruler of the people, and as chief of the human kings.

6. Superior art thou, inferior are thy rivals, and whatsoever adversaries are thine, O king! Sole ruler, befriended of Indra, victorious, bring thou hither the supplies of those who act as thy enemies!

7. Presenting the front of a lion do thou devour all (their) people, present-ing the front of a tiger do thou strike down the enemies! Sole ruler, befriended of Indra, victorious, seize upon the supplies of those who act as thy enemies!

I, 9. Prayer for earthly and heavenly success

1. Upon this (person) the Vasus, Indra, Pûshan, Varuna, Mitra, and Agni, shall bestow goods (vasu)! The Âdityas, and, further, all the gods shall hold him in the higher light!

2. Light, ye gods, shall be at his bidding: Sûrya (the sun), Agni (fire), or even gold! Inferior to us shall be our rivals! Cause him to ascend to the highest heaven

3. With that most potent charm with which, O Gâtavedas (Agni), thou didst bring to Indra the (soma-) drink, with that, O Agni, do thou here strengthen this one; grant him supremacy over his kinsmen!

4. Their sacrifice and their glory, their increase of wealth and their thoughtful plans, I have usurped, O Agni. Inferior to us shall be our rivals! Cause him to ascend to the highest heaven!

VI, 38. Prayer for lustre and power

1. The brilliancy that is in the lion, the tiger, and the serpent; in Agni, the Brâhmana, and Surya (shall be ours)! May the lovely goddess that bore Indra come to us, endowed with lustre!

2. (The brilliancy) that is in the elephant, panther, and in gold; in the waters, cattle, and men (shall be ours)! May the lovely goddess that bore Indra come to us, endowed with lustre!

3. (The brilliancy) that is in the chariot, the dice, in the strenath of the bull; in the wind, Parganya, and in the fire of Varuna (shall be ours)! May the lovely goddess that bore Indra come to us, endowed with lustre!

4. (The brilliancy) that is in the man of royal caste, in the stretched drum, in the strength of the horge, in the shout of men (shall be ours)! May the lovely goddess that bore Indra come to us, endowed with lustre!

VI, 39. Prayer for glory (yasas)

1. The oblation that yields glory, sped on by Indra, of thousandfold strength, well offered, prepared with might, shall prosper! Cause me, that offers the oblation, to continue long beholding (light), and to rise to supremacy!

2. (That he may come) to us, let us honour with obeisance glory-owning Indra, the glorious one with glory-yielding (oblations)! Do thou (the oblation) grant us sovereignty sped on by Indra; may we in thy favour be glorious!

3. Glorious was Indra born, glorious Agni, glorious Soma. Glorious, of all beings the most glorious, am I.

VIII, 8. Battle-charm

1. May Indra churn (the enemy), he, the churner, Sakra (mighty), the hero, that pierces the forts, so that we shall slay the armies of the enemies a thousandfold!

2. May the rotten rope, wafting itself against yonder army, turn it into a stench. When the enemies see from afar our smoke and fire, fear shall they lay into their hearts!

3. Tear asunder those (enemies), O asvattha (ficus religiosa), devour (khâda) them, O! khadira (acacia catechu) in lively style! Like the tâgadbhanga (ricinus communis) they shall be broken (bhagyantâm), may the vadhaka (a certain kind of tree) slay them with his weapons (vadhaih)!

4. May the knotty âhva-plant put knots upon yonder (enemies), may the vadhaka slay them with his weapons! Bound up in (our) great trap-net, they shall quickly be broken as an arrow-reed!

5. The atmosphere was the net, the great regions (of space) the (supporting) poles of the net: with these Sakra (mighty Indra) did surround and scatter the army of the Dasyus.

6. Great, forsooth, is the net of great Sakra, who is rich in steeds: with it infold thou all the enemies, so that not one of them shall be released!

7. Great is the net of thee, great Indra, hero, that art equal to a thousand, and hast hundredfold might. With that (net) Sakra slew a hundred, thousand, ten thousand, a hundred million foes, having surrounded them with (his) army.

8. This great world was the net of great Sakra: with this net of Indra I infold all those (enemies) yonder in darkness,

9. With great dejection, failure, and irrefragable misfortune; with fatigue, lassitude, and confusion, do I surround all those (enemies) yonder.

10. To death do I hand them over, with the fetters of death they have been bound. To the evil messengers of death do I lead them captive.

11. Guide ye those (foes), ye messengers of death; ye messengers of Yama, infold them! Let more than thousands be slain; may the club of Bhava crush them!

12. The Sâdhyas (blessed) go holding up with might one support of the net, the Rudras another, the Vasus another, (Still) another is upheld by the Âdityas.

13. All the gods shall go pressing from above with might; the Angiras shall go on the middle (of the net), slaying the mighty army!

14. The trees, and (growths) that are like trees, the plants and the herbs as well; two-footed and four-footed creatures do I impel, that they shall slay yonder army!

15. The Gandharvas and Apsaras, the serpents and the gods, holy men and (deceased) Fathers, the visible and invisible (beings), do I impel, that they shall slay yonder army!

16. Scattered here are the fetters of death; when thou steppest upon them thou shalt not escape! May this hammer slay (the men) of yonder army by the thousand!

17. The gharma (sacrificial hot drink) that has been heated by the fire, this sacrifice (shall) slay thousands! Do ye, Bhava and Sarva, whose arms are mottled, slay yonder army!

18. Into the (snare of) death they shall fall, into hunger, exhaustion, slaughter, and fear! O Indra and Sarva, do ye with trap and net slay yonder army!

19. Conquered, O foes, do ye flee away; repelled by (our) charm, do ye run! Of yonder host, repulsed by Brihaspati, not one shall be saved!

20. May their weapons fall from their (hands), may they be unable to lay the arrow on (the bow)! And then (our) arrows shall smite them, badly frightened, in their vital members!

21. Heaven and earth shall shriek at them, and the atmosphere, along with the divine powers! Neither aider, nor support did they find; smiting one another they shall go to death!

22. The four regions are the she-mules of the god's chariot, the purodâsas (sacrificial rice-cakes) the hoofs, the atmosphere the seat (of the wagon). Heaven and earth are its two sides, the seasons the reins, the intermediate regions the attendants, Vâk (speech) the road.

23. The year is the chariot, the full year is the body of the chariot, Virâg, the pole, Agni the front part of the chariot. Indra is the (combatant) standing on the left of the chariot, Kandramas (the moon) the charioteer.

24. Do thou win here, do thou conquer here, overcome, win, hail! These here shall conquer, those yonder be conquered! Hail to these here, perdition to those yonder! Those yonder do I envelop in blue and red!

I, 19. Battle-charm against arrow-wounds

1. The piercing (arrows) shall not hit us, nor shall the striking arrows hit us! Far away fron, us O Indra, to either side, cause the arrow-shower to fall!

2. To either side of us the arrows shall fall, those that have been shot and shall be shot! Ye divine and ye human arrows, pierce ye mine enemies!

3. Be he our own, or be he strange, the kinsman, or the foreianer, who bear enmity towards us, those enemies of mine Rudra shall pierce with a shower of arrows!

4. Him that rivals us, or does not rival us, him that curses us with hate, may all the gods injure my charm protects me from within!

III, 1. Battle-charm for confusing the enemy

1. Agni shall skilfully march against our opponents, burning against their schemes and hostile plans; Gâtavedas shall confuse the army of our opponents and deprive them (of the use) of their hands!

2. Ye Maruts are mighty in such matters: advance ye, crush ye, conquer ye (the enerny)! These Vasus when implored did crush (them). Agni, vily, as their vanauard shall skilfully attack!

3. O Maghavan, the hostile army which contends against us--do ye, O Indra, Vritra's slayer, and Agni, burn against them!

4. Thy thunderbolt, O Indra, who hast been driven forward swiftly by thy two bay steeds, shall advance, crushing the enemies. Slay them that resist, pursue, or flee, deprive their schemes of fulfilment!

5. O Indra, confuse the army of the enemy; with the impact of the fire and the wind scatter them to either side!

6. Indra shall confuse the army, the Miaruts shall slay it with might! Agni shall rob it of its sight; vanquished it shall turn about!

III, 2. Battle-charm for confusing the enemy

1. Agni, our skilful vanguard, shall attack, burning, against their schemes and hostile plans! Gâtavedas shall bewilder the plans of the enemy, and deprive them (of the use) of their hands!

2. This fire has confused the schemes that are in your mind; it shall blow you from your home, blow you away from everywhere!

3. O Indra, bewildering their schemes, come hither with thy (own) plan: with the impact of the fire and the wind scatter them to either side!

4. O ye plans of theirs, fly ye away; O ye schemes, be ye confused! Moreover, what now is in their mind, do thou drive that out of them!

5. Do thou, O (goddess) Apvi, confusing their plans, go forth (to them), and seize their limbs! Attack them, burn with flames into their hearts; strike the enemy with fits, (strike our) opponents with darkness!

6. That army yonder o(the enemy, that comes against us fighting with might, do ye, O Maruts, strike with planless darkness, that one of them shall not know the other!

VI, 97. Battle-charm of a king upon the eve of battle

1. Superior is the sacrifice, superior Agni, superior Soma, superior Indra. To the end that I shall be superior to all hostile armies do we thus, offering the agnihotra, reverently present this oblation!

2. Hail be, ye wise Mitra and Varuna: with honey swell ye our kingdom here, (so that it shall) abound in offspring! Drive far to a distance misfortune, strip off from us sin, even after it has been committed!

3. With inspiration follow ye this strong hero; cling close, ye friends, to Indra (the king), who conquers villages, conquers cattle, has the thunderbolt in his arm, overcomes the host arrayed (against him), crushing it with might!

VI, 99. Battle-charm of a king on the eve of battle

1. I call -upon thee, O Indra, from afar, upon thee for protection against tribulation. I call the strong avenger that has many names, and is of unequalled birth.

2. Where the hostile weapon now rises against us,threatening to slay, there do we place the two arms of Indra round about.

3. The two arms of Indra, the protector, do we place round about us: let him protect us! O god Savitar, and king Soma, render me of confident mind, that I may prosper!

XI, 9. Prayer to Arbudi and Nyarbudi for help in battle

1. The arms, the arrows, and the might of the bows; the swords, the axes, the weapons, and the artful scheme that is in our mind; all that, O Arbudi, do thou make the enemies see, and spectres also make them see!

2. Arise, and arm yourselves; friends are ye, O divine folk! May our friends be perceived and protected by you, O Arbudi (and Nyarbudi)!

3. Arise (ye two), and take hold! With fetters and shackles surround ye the armies of the enemy, O Arbudi (and Nyarbudi)!

4. The god whose name is Arbudi, and the lord Nyarbudi, by whom the atmosphere and this great earth has been infolded, with these two companions of Indra do I pursue the conquered (king) with my army.

5. Arise, thou divine person, O Arbudi, together with thy army! Crushing the army of tlie enemy, encompass them with thy embraces!

6. Thou, Arbudi, makest appear the sevenfold spectral brood. Do thou, when the oblation has been poured, rise up with all. these, together with the army!

7. (The female mourner), beating herself, with tear-stained face, with short (mutilated?) ears, with dishevelled hair, shall lament, when a man has been slain, pierced by thee, O Arbudi!

8. She curves her spine while longing in her heart for her son, her husband, and her kin, when (a man) has been pierced by thee, O Arbudi!

9. The aliklavas and the gâshkamadas, the vultures, the strong-winged hawks, the crows, and the birds (of prey) shall obtain their fill! Let them make evident to the enemy, when (a man) has been pierced by thee, O Arbudi!

10. Then, too, every wild beast, insect, and worm shall obtain his fill on the human carcass, when (a man) has been pierced by thee, O Arbudi!

11. Seize ye, and tear out in-breathing and outbreathing, O Nyarbudi (and Arbudi): deep-sounding groans shall arise! Let them make it evident to the enemy, when (a man) has been pierced by thee, O Arbudi!

12. Scare them forth, let them tremble; bewilder the enemies with fright! With thy broad embrace, with the clasp of thy arms crush the enemies, O Nyarbudi!

13. May their arms, and the artful scheme that is in their mind be confused! Not a thing shall remain of them, pierced by thee, O Arbudi!

14. May (the mourning women) beating them selves, run together, smiting their breasts and their thighs, not anointed, with dishevelled hair, howling, when a man has been slain, has been pierced by thee, O Arbudi!

15. The dog-like Apsaras, and also the Rûpakâs (phantoms), the plucking sprite, that eacerly licks within the vessel, and her that seeks out what has been carelessly hidden, all those do thou, O Arbudi, make the enemies see, and spectres also make them see!

16. (And also make them see) her that strides upon the mist, the mutilated one, who dwells with the mutilated; the vapoury spooks that are hidden, and the Gandharvas and Apsaras, the serpents, and other brood, and the Rakshas!

17. (And also) the spooks with fourfold teeth, black teeth, testicles like a pot, bloody faces, who are inherently frightful, and terrifying!

18. Frighten thou, O Arbudi, yonder lines of the enemy; the conquering and the victorious (Arbudi and Nyarbudi), the two comrades of Indra, shall conquer the enemies!

19. Dissolved, crushed, slain the enemy shall lie, O Nyarbudi! May victorious sprites, with fiery tongues and smoky crests, go with (our) army!

20. Of the enemies repulsed by this (army), O Arbudi, Indra, the spouse of Saki, shall slay each picked man: not a single one of those yonder shall escape!

21. May their hearts burst, may their life's breath escape upward! May dryness of the mouth overtake (our) enemies, but not (our) allies!

22. Those who are bold and those who are cowardly, those who turn (in flight) and those who are deaf (to danger?), those who are (like) dark goats, and those, too, who bleat like goats, all those, do thou, O Arbudi, make the enemies see, and spectres also make them see!

23. Arbudi and Trishamdhi shall pierce our enemies, so that, O Indra, slayer of Vritra, spouse of Sakî, we may slay the enemy by thousands!

24. The trees, and (growths) that are like trees, the plants and the herbs as well, the Gandharvas and the Apsaras, the serpents, gods, pious men, and (departed) Fathers, all those, O Arbudi, do thou make the enemies see, and spectres also make them see!

25. The Maruts, god Âditya, Brahmanaspati did rule over you; Indra, and Agni, Dhâtar, Mitra, and Pragâpati did rule over you; the seers did rule over you. Let them make evident to the enemies when (a man) has been pierced by thee, O Arbudi!

26. Ruling over all these, rise ye and arm yourselves! Ye divine folk are (our) friends: win ye the battle, and disperse to your various abodes!

XI, 10. Prayer to Trishamdhi for help in battle

1. Arise and arm yourselves, ye nebulous spectres together with fiery portents; ye serpents, other brood, and Rakshas, run ye after the enemy!

2. He knows bow to rule your kingdom together with the red portents (of the heavens). The evil brood that is in the air and the heaven, and the human (powers) upon the earth, shall be obedient to the plans of Tri-shamdhi!

3. The brazen-beaked (birds of prey), those with beaks pointed as a needle, and those, too, with thorny beaks, flesh-devouring, swift as the wind, shall fasten themselves upon the enemies, together with the Trishamdhi-bolt (the bolt with three joints)!

4. Make away with, O Gâtavedas Âditya, many carcasses! This army of Trishamdhi shall be devoted to my bidding!

5. Arise thou divine person, O Arbudi, together with thy army! This tribute has been offered to you (Arbudi and Trishamdhi), an offerinor pleasing to Trishamdhi.

6. This white-footed, four-footed arrow shall fetter (?). Do thou, O magic spell, operate, together with the army of Trishamdhi, against the enemies!

7. May (the mourning woman) with suffused eyes hurry on, may she that hath short (mutilated?) ears shout when (a man) has been overcome by the army of Trishamdhi! Red portents shall be (visible)!

8. May the winged birds that move in the air and in the sky descend; beasts of prey and insects shall seize upon them; the vultures that feed upon raw flesh shall hack into (their) carcasses!

9. By virtue of the compact which thou, O Brihaspati, didst close with Indra and Brahman, by virtue of that agreement with Indra, do I call hither all the gods: on this side conquer, not over yonder!

10. Brihaspati, the descendant of Angiras, and the seers, inspired by (our) song, did fix the three-jointed (Trishamdhi) weapon upon the sky for the destruction of the Asuras.

11. Trishamdhi, by whom both yonder Âditya (the sun) and Indra, are protected, the gods did destine for (our) might and strencth.

12. All the worlds the gods did conquer through this oblation, (and) by the bolt which Brihaspati, the descendant of Angiras, did mould into a weapon for the destruction of the Asuras.

13. With the bolt which Brihaspati, the descendant of Angiras, did, mould into a weapon for the destruction of the Asuras do I, O Brihaspati, annihilate yonder army: I smite the enemies with force.

14. All the gods that eat the oblation offered with the call vashat are coming over. Receive this oblation graciously; conquer on this side, not over yonder!

15. May all the gods come over: the oblation is pleasing to Trishamdhi. Adhere to the great compact under which of yore the Asuras were conquered!

16. Vâyu (the wind) shall bend the points of the enemies' bows, Indra shall break their arms, so that they shall be unable to lay on their arrows, Âditya (the sun) shall send their missiles astray, and Kandramas (the moon) shall bar the way of (the enemy) that has not (as yet) started!

17. If they have come on as citadels of the gods, if they have constituted an inspired charm as their armour, if they have gathered courage through the protections for the body and the bulwarks which they have made, render all that devoid of force!

18. Placing (our) purohita (chaplain), together with the flesh-devourer (Agni) and death, in thy train, do thoti, O Trishamdhi, go forth with thy army, conquer the enemies, advance!

19. O Trishamdhi, envelop thou the enemies in darkness; may not a single one of those, driven forth by the speckled ghee, be saved!

20. May the white-footed (arrow?) fly to yonder lines of the enemy, may yonder armies of the enemies be to-day put to confusion, O Nyarbudi!

21. The enemies have been confused, O Nyarbudi: slay each picked man among them, slay them with this army!

22. The enemy with coat-of-mail, he that has no coat-of-mail, and he that stands in the battle-throng, throttled by the strings of their bows, by the fastenings of their coats-of-mail, by the battle-throng, they shall lie!

23. Those w ith armour and those without armour, the enemies that are shielded by armour, all those, O Arbudi, after they have been slain, dogs shall devour upon the ground!

24. Those that ride on chariots, and those that have no chariots, those that are mounted, and those that are not mounted, all those, after they have been slain, vultures and strong-winged hawks shall devour!

25. Counting its dead by thousands, the hostile army, pierced and shattered in the clash of arms, shall lie!

26. Pierced in a vital spot, shrieking in concert with the birds of prey, wretched, crushed, prostrate, (the birds of prey) shall devour the enemy who attempts to hinder this oblation of ours directed against (him)!

27. With (the oblation) to which the gods flock, which is free from failure,- with it Indra, the slayer of Vritra, shall slay, and with the Trishamdhi-bolt (the bolt with three joints)!

V, 20. Hymn to the battle-drum

1. High sounds the voice of the drum, that acts the warrior, the wooden (drum), equipped with the skin of the cow. Whetting thy voice, subduing the enemy, like a lion sure of victory, do thou loudly thunder against them!

2. The wooden (instrument) with fastened (covering) has thundered as a lion, as a bull roars to the cow that longs to mate. Thou art a bull, thy enemies are eunuchs; thou ownest Indra's foesubduing fire!

3. Like a bull in the herd, full of might, lusty, do thou, O snatcher of booty, roar against them! Pierce with fire the heart of the enemy; with -broken ranks the foe shall run and scatter!

4. In victorious battles raise thy roar! What may be captured, capture; sound in many places! Favour, O drum, (our deeds) with thy divine voice; bring to (us) with strength the property of the enemy!

5. When the wife of the enemy hears the voice of the drum, that speaks to a far distance, may she, aroused by the sound, distressed, snatch her son to her arms, and run, frightened at the clash of arms!

6. Do thou, O drum, sound the first sound, ring brilliantly over the back of the earth! Open wide thy maw at the enemies host; resound brightly, joyously, O drum!

7. Between this heaven and earth thy noise shall spread, thy sounds shall quickly part to every side! Shout thou and thunder with swelling sound; make music at thy friend's victory, having, (chosen) the good side!

8. Manipulated with care, its voice shall resound! Make bristle forth the weapons of the warriors! Allied to Indra do thou call hither the warriors; with thy friends beat vigorously down the enemies!

9. A shouting herald, followed by a bold army, spreading news in many places, sounding through the village, eager for success, knowing the way, do thou distribute glory to many in the battle!

10. Desiring advantage, gaining booty, full mighty, thou hast been made keen by (my) song, and winnest battles. As the press-stone on the gathering skin dances upon the soma-sboots, thus do thou, O drum, lustily dance upon the booty!

11. A conqueror of enemies, overwhelming, foe-subduing, eager for the fray, victoriously crushing, as a speaker his speech do thou carry forth thy sound; sound forth here strength for victory in battle!

12. Shaking those that are unshaken, hurrying to the strife, a conqueror of enemies, an unconquerable leader, protected by Indra, attending to the hosts, do thou that crusheth the hearts of the enemies, quickly go!

V, 21 Hymn to the battle-drum, the terror of the enemy

1. Carry with thy voice, O drum, lack of heart, and failure of courage among the enemies! Disagreement, dismay, and fright, do we place into the enemies: beat them down, O drum!

2. Agitated in their minds, their sight, their hearts, the enemies shall run, frightened with terror, when our oblation has been offered!

3. Made of wood, equipped with the skin of the cow, at home with every clan, put thou with thy voice terror into the enemies, when thou hast been anointed with ghee!

4. As the wild animals of the forest start in fear from man, thus do thou, O drum, shout against the enemies, frighten them away, and bewilder their minds!

5. As goats and sheep run from the wolf, badly frightened, thus do thou, O drum, shout against the enemies, frighten them away, and bewilder their minds!

6. As birds start in fear from the eagle, as by day and by night (they start) at the roar of the lion, thus do thou, O drum, shout against the enemies, frighten them away, and bewilder their minds!

7. With the drum and the skin of the antelope all the gods, that sway the battle, have scared away the enemies.

8. At the noise of the beat of the feet when Indra disports himself, and at his shadow, our enemies yonder, that come in successive ranks, shall tremble!

9. The whirring of the bowstring and the drums shall shout at the directions where the conquered armies of the enemies go in successive ranks!

10. O sun, take away their sight; O rays, run after them; clinging to their feet, fasten yourselves upon them, when the strength of their arms is gone!

11. Ye strong Maruts, Prisni's children, with Indra as an ally, crush ye the enemies; Soma the king (shall crush them), Varuna the king, Mahâdeva, and

also Mrityu (death), and Indra!
12. These wise armies of the gods, having the sun as their ensign, shall conquer our enemies! Hail!

CHARMS TO SECURE HARMONY, INFLUENCE IN THE ASSEMBLY, AND THE LIKE (SÂMMANASYÂNI, ETC.).

III, 30. Charm to secure harmony

1. Unity of heart, and unity of mind, freedom from hatred, do I procure for you. Do ye take delight in one another, as a cow in her (new-) born calf!

2. The son shall be devoted to his father, be of the same mind with his mother; the wife shall speak honied, sweet, words to her husband!

3. The brother shall not hate the brother, and the sister not the sister! Harmonious, devoted to the same purpose, speak ye words in kindly spirit!

4. That charm which causes the gods not to disagree, and not to hate one another, that do we prepare in your house, as a means of agreement for your folk.

5. Following your leader, of (the same) mind, do ye not hold yourselves apart! Do ye come here, co-operating, going along the same wagon-pole, speaking agreeably to one another! I render you of the same aim, of the same mind.

6. Identical shall be your drink, in common shall be your share of food! I yoke you together in the same traces: do ye worship Agni, joining together, as spokes around about the hub!

7. I render you of the same aim, of the same mind, all paying deference to one (person) through my harmonising charm. Like the gods that are guarding the ambrosia, may he (the leader) be welldisposed towards you, night and day!

VI, 73. Charm to allay discord

1. Hither shall come Varuna, Soma, Agni; Brihaspati with the Vasus shall come hither! Come together, O ye kinsmen all, of one mind, to the glory of this mighty guardian!

2. The fire that is within your souls, the scheme that hath entered your minds, do I frustrate with my oblation, with my ghee: delight in me shall ye take, O kinsmen!

3. Remain right here, go not away from us; (the roads) at a distance Pûshan shall make impassable for you! Vistoshpati shall urgently call you back: delight in me shall ye take, O kinsmen!

VI, 74. Charm to allay discord

1. May your bodies be united, may your mindg and your purposes (be united)! Brahmanaspati here has brought you together, Bhaga has brought you together.

2. Harmony of mind (I procure) for you, and also harmony of heart. Moreover with the aid of Bhaga's exertions do I cause you to agree.

3. As the Âdityas are united with the Vasus, as the fierce (Rudras), free from grudge, with the Maruts, thus, O three-named (Agni), without grudge, do thou render these people here of the same mind!

VII, 52. Charm against strife and bloodshed

1. May we be in harmony with our kinfolk, in harmony with strangers; do ye, O Asvins, establish here agreement among us!

2. May we agree in mind and thought, may we not struggle with one another, in a spirit displeasing to the gods! Ma not the din of frequent battle-carnage arise, may the arrow not fly when the day of Indra has arrived!

VI, 64. Charm to allay discord

1. Do ye agree, unite yourselves, may your minds be in harmony, just as the gods of old in harmony-. sat down to their share!

2. Same be their counsel, same their assembly, same their aim, in common their thought! The 'same' oblation do I sacrifice for you: do ye enter upon the same plan!

Same be your intention, same your hearts! Same be your mind, so that it may be perfectly in common to you!

VI, 42. Charm to appease anger

1. As the bowstring from the bow, thus do I take off thy anger from thy heart, so that, having become of the same mind, we shall associate like friends!

2. Like friends we shall associate-I take off thy anger. Under a stone that is heavy do we cast thy anger.
3. I step upon thy anger with my heel and my fore-foot, so that, bereft of will, thou shalt not speak, shalt come up to my wish!

VI, 43. Charm to appease anger

1. This darbha-grass removes the anger of both kinsman and of stranger. And this remover of wrath, 'appeaser of wrath' it is called.

2. This darbha-grass of many roots, that reaches down into the ocean, having risen from the earth, 'appeaser of wrath' it is called.

3. Away we take the offensiveness that is in thy jaw, away (the offensiveness) in thy mouth, so that, bereft of will, thou shalt not speak, shalt come up to my wish!

II, 27. Charm against opponents in debate, undertaken with the pâtâ-plant

1. May the enemy not win the debate! Thou art mighty and overpowering. Overcome the debate of those that debate against us, render them devoid of force, O plant!

2. An eagle found thee out, a boar dug thee out with his snout. Overcome the debate of those that debate against us, render them devoid of force, O plant!

3. Indra placed thee upon his arm in order to overthrow the Asuras. Overcome the debate of those that debate against us, render them devoid of force, O plant!

4. Indra did eat the pâtâ-plant, in order to overthrow the Asuras. Overcome the debate of those that debate against us, render them devoid of force, O plant!

5. By means of thee I shall conquer the enemy, as Indra (conquered) the Sâlâvrikas. Overcome the debate of those that debate against us, render them devoid of force, O plant!

6. O Rudra, whose remedy is the urine, with black crest of hair, performer of (strong) deeds,overcome thou the debate of those that debate against us, render them devoid of force, O plant!

7. Overcome thou the debate of him that is hostile to us, O Indra! Encourage us with thy might! Render me superior in debate!

VII, 12. Charm to procure influence in the assembly

1. May assembly and meeting, the two daughters of Pragâpati, concurrently aid me! May he with whom I shall meet co-operate with me, may I, O ye Fathers, speak agreeably to those assembled!

2. We know thy name, O assembly: 'mirth,' verily, is thy name; may all those that sit assembled in thee utter speech in harmony with me!

3. Of them that are sitting together I take to myself the power and the understanding: in this entire vathering render, O Indra, me successful!

4. If your mind has wandered to a distance, or has been enchained here or there, then do we turn it hither: may your mind take delight in me!

VI, 94. Charm to bring about submission to one's will

1. Your minds, your purposes, your plans, do we cause to bend. Ye persons yonder, that are devoted to other purposes, we cause you to comply!

2. With my mind do I seize your minds: do ye with your thoughts follow my thought! I place your hearts in my control: come ye, directing your way after my course!

3. I have called upon heaven and earth, I have called upon the goddess Sarasvatî, I have called upon both Indra and Agni: may we succeed in this. O Sarasvatî!

CHARMS TO SECURE PROSPERITY IN HOUSE, FIELD, CATTLE, BUSINESS, GAMBLING, AND KINDRED MATTERS

III, 12. Prayer at the building of a house

1. Right here do I erect a firm house: may it stand upon a (good) foundation, dripping with ghee! Thee may we inhabit, O house, with heroes all, with strong heroes, with uninjured heroes!

2. Right here, do thou, O house, stand firmly, full of horses, full of cattle, full of abundance! Full of sap, ful.] of ghee, full of milk, elevate thyself unto great happiness!

3. A supporter art thou, O house, with broad roof, containing purified grain! To thee may the calf come, to thee the child, to thee the milch-cows, when they return in the evening!

4. May Savitar, Vâyu, Indra, Brihaspati cunningly erect this house! Alay the Alaruts sprinkle it with moisture and with ghee; may king Bhaga let our ploughing take root!

5. O mistress of dwelling, as a sheltering and kindly goddess thou wast erected by the gods in the bealrinina; clothed in grass, be thou kindly disposed; give us, moreover, wealth along with heroes!

6. Do thou, O cross-beam, according to regulation ascend the post, do thou, mightily ruling, hold off the enemies! May they that approach thee reverently, O house, not suffer injury, may we with all our heroes live a hundred autumns!

7. Hither to this (house) hath come the tender child, hither the calf along with (the other) domestic animals; hither the vessel (full) of liquor, together with bowls of sour milk!

8. Carry forth, O woman, this full jar, a stream of ghee mixed with ambrosia! Do thou these drinkers supply with ambrosia; the sacrifice and the gifts (to the Brahmans) shall it (the house) protect!

9. These waters, free from disease, destructive of disease, do I carry forth. The chambers do I enter in upon together with the immortal Agni (fire).

VI, 142. Blessing during the sowing of seed

1. Raise thyself up, grow thick by thy own might, O grain! Burst every vessel! The lightning in the heavens shall not destroy thee!

2. When we invoke thee, god grain, and thou dost listen, then do thou raise thyself up like the sky, be inexhaustible as the sea!

3. Inexhaustible shall be those that attend to thee, inexhaustible thy heaps! Theywhogivethee as a present shall be inexhaustible, they who eat thee shall be inexhaustible!

VI, 79. Charm for procuring increase of grain

1. May this bounteous Nabhasaspati (the lord of the cloud) preserve for us (possessions) without measure in our house!

2. Do thou, O Nabhasaspati, keep strengthening food in our house, may prosperity and goods come hither!

3. O bounteous god, thou dost command thousandfold prosperity: of that do thou bestow upon iis, of that do thou give us, in that may we share with thee!

VI, 50. Exorcism of vermin infesting grain in the field

1. Slay ye the tarda ('borer'), the samanka ('hook'), and the mole, O Asvins; cut off their heads, and crush their ribs! Shut their mouths, that they shall not eat the barley; free ye, moreover, the grain from danger!

2. Ho tarda ('borer'), ho locust, ho gabhya ('snapper'), upakvasa! As a Brahman (eats not) an uncompleted sacrifice, do ye, not eating this barley, without working injury, get out!

3. O husband of the tardâ (-female), O husband Of the vaghâ (-female), ye of the sharp teeth, listen to me! The vyadvaras ('rodents') of the forest, and whatever other vyadvaras (there are), all these we do crush.

VII, 11. Charm to protect grain from lightning

1. With thy broad thunder,with the beacon, elevated by the gods that pervade this all, with the lightning do thou not destroy our grain, O god; nor do thou destroy it with the rays of the sun!

II, 26. Charm for the prosperity of cattle

1. Hither shall come the cattle which have strayed to a distance, whose companionship Vâyu (the wind) enjoys! (The cattle) whose structure of form Tvashtar knows, Savitar shall hold in place in this stable!

2. To this stable the cattle shall flow together, Brihaspati skilfully shall conduct them hither! Sînîvâlî shall conduct hither their van: do thou, O Anumati, hold them in place after they have arrived!

3. May the cattle, may the horses, and may the domestics flow together; may the increase of the grain flow together! I sacrifice with an oblation that causeth to flow together!

4. I pour together the milk of the cows, I pour together strength and sap with the ghee. Poured together shall be our heroes, constant shall be the cows with me the owner of the cows!

5. I bring hither the milk of the cows, I have brought hither the sap of the grain. Brought hither are our heroes, brought hither to this house are our wives.

III, 14. Charm for the prosperity of cattle

1. With a firmly founded stable, with wealth, with well-being, with the name of that which is born on a lucky day do we unite you (O cattle)!

2. May Aryaman unite you, may Pûshan, Brihaspati, and Indra, the conqueror of booty, unite you! Do ye prosper my possessions!

Flocking together without fear, making ordure in this stable, holding honey fit for soma, free from disease, ye shall come hither!

4. Right here come, ye cows, and prosper here like the sakâ-bird! And right here do ye beget (your youn(y)! May ye be in accord with me!

5. May your stable be auspicious to you, prosper ye like the sâri-birds and parrots! And right here do ye beget (your young)! With us do we unite you.

6. Attach yourselves, O cows, to me as your possessor; may this stable here cause you to prosper! Upon you, growing numerous, and living, may we, increasing in wealth, alive, attend!

VI, 59. Prayer to the plant arundhatî for protection to cattle

1. Thy foremost protection, O Arundhatî, do thou bestow upon steer and milch-kine, upon (cattle of) the age when weaned from their mother, upon (all) four-footed creatures!

2. May Arundhatî, the herb, bestow protection along with the gods, render full of sap the stable, free from disease our men!

3. The variegated, lovely, life-giving (plant) do I invoke. May she carry away for us, far from the cattle, the missile hurled by Rudra!

VI, 70. Charm to secure the attachment of a cow to her calf

1. As meat, and liquor, and dice (abound) at the gambling-place, as the heart of thf. lusty male hankers after the woman, thus shall thy heart, O cow, hanker after the calf!

2. As the elephant directs his steps after the steps of the female, as the heart of the lusty male hankers after the woman, thus shall thy heart, O cow, hanker after the calf!

3. As the felloe, and as the spokes, and as the nave (of the wheel is joined) to the felloe, as the heart of the lusty male hankers after the woman, thus shall thy heart, O cow, hanker after the calf!

III, 28. Formula in expiation of the birth of twin-calves

1. Through one creation at a time this (cow) was born, when the fashioners of the beings did create the cows of many colours. (Therefore), when a cow doth beget twins portentously, growling and cross she injureth the cattle.

2. This (cow) doth injure our cattle: a flesh-eater, devourer, she hath become. Hence to a Brahman he shall give her; in this way she may be kindly and auspicious!

3. Auspicious be to (our) men, auspicious to (our) cows and horses, auspicious to this entire field, auspicious be to us right here!

4. Here be prosperity, licre be sap! Be thou here one that especially gives a thousandfold! Make the cattle prosper, thou mother of twins!

5. Where our pious friends live joyously, having left behind the ailments of their bodies, to that world the mother of twins did attain: may she not injure our men and our cattle!

6. Where is the world of our pious friends, where the world of thern that sacrifice with the agnihotra, to that world the mother of twins did attain: may she not injure our imen and our cattle!

VI, 92. Charm to endow a horse with swiftness

1. Swift as the wind be thou, O steed, when joined (to the chariot); at Indra's urging go, fleet as the mind! The Maruts, the all-possessing, shall harness thee,Tvashtar shall put fleetness into thy feet!

2. With the fleetness, O runner, that has been deposited in thee in a secret place, (with the fleetness) that has been made over to the eagle, the wind, and moves in them, with that, O steed, strong with strength, do thou win the. race, reaching the goal in the contest!

3. Thy body, O steed, leading (our) body, shall run, a pleasure to ourselves, delight to thyself! A god, not stumbling, for the support of the great, he shall, as if upon the heaven, found his own light!

III, 13. Charm for conducting a river into a new channel

1. Because of yore, when the (cloud-) serpent was slain (by Indra), ye did rush forth and shout (anadatâ), therefore is your name 'shouters' (nadyah rivers'): that is your designation, ye streams!

2. Because, when sent forth by Varuna, ye then quickly did bubble up; then Indra met (âpnot) you, as ye went, therefore anon are ye 'meeters' (âpah waters')!

3. When reluctantly ye flowed, Indra, forsooth, did with might choose (avîvarata) you as his own, ye goddesses! Therefore 'choice' (vâr 'water') has been given you as your name!

4. One god stood upon you, as ye flowed according to will. Up breathed (ud ânishuh) they who are known as 'the great' (mahîh). Therefore 'upbreather' (udakam 'water') are they called!

5. The waters are kindly, the waters in truth were ghee. These waters, truly, do support Agni and Soma. May the readily flowing, strong sap of the honey-dripping (waters) come to me, together with life's breath and lustre!

6. Then do I see them and also do I hear them; their sound, their voice doth come to me. When, ye golden-coloured, I have refreshed myself with you, then I ween, ambrosia (amrita) am I tasting!

7. Here, ye waters, is your heart, here is your calf, ye righteous ones! Come ye, mighty ones, by this way here, by which I am conducting you here!

VI, 106. Charm to ward off danger from fire

1. Where thou comest, (O fire), and where thou goest away, the blooming dûrvâ-plant shall grow: a well-spring there shall rise up, or a lotus-laden pool!

2. Here (shall be) the gathering place of the waters, here the dwelling-place of the sea! In the midst of a pond our house shall be: turn, (O fire), away thy jaws!

With a covering of coolness do we envelop thee, O house; cool as a pond be thou for us! Agni shall furnish the remedy!

IV, 3. Shepherd's charm against wild beasts and robbers

1. Three have gone away from here, the tiger, man, and wolf. Out of sight, forsooth, cm the rivers, out of siaht (grows the divine tree (the banyan-tree?): out of sight the enemies shall retreat!

2. The wolf shall tlead a distant path, and the robber one still more distant! On a distant path shall move the biting rope (the serpent), on a distant path the plotter of evil!

3. Thy eyes and thy jaw we crush, O tiger, and also all thy twenty claws.
4. We crush the tiger, the foremost of animals, armed with teeth. Next, too, the thief, and then the serpent, the wizard, and also the wolf.

5. The thief that approacheth to-day, crushed to pieces he goeth away. Where the paths are precipitate he shall go, Indra shall slay him with his bolt!

6. The teeth of the wild beast are dulled, and broken are his ribs. Out of thy sight the dragon shall go, down shall tumble the hare-hunting beast!

7. The (jaw, O beast,) that thou shuttest together, thou shalt not open up; that which thou openest up, thou shalt not shut together!--Born of Indra, born of Soma, thou, (my charm), art Atharvan's crusher of tigers.

III, 15. A merchant's prayer

1. Indra, the merchant, do I summon: may he come to us, may he be our van; driving away the demon of grudge, the waylayers, and wild beasts, may he, the possessor, bestow wealth upon me!

2. May the many paths, the roads of the gods, which come together between heaven and earth, c,ladden me with milk and ghee, so that I may gather in wealth from my purchases!

3. Desirous do I, O Agni, with firewood and ghee offer oblations (to thee), for success and strength; according to ability praising (thee) with my prayer, do I sing this divine song, that I may gain a hundredfold!

4. (Pardon, O Agni, this sin of ours [incurred upon] the far road which we have travelled!) May our purchases and our sales be successful for us; may what I get in barter render me a gainer! May ye two (Indra and Agni) in accord take pleasure in this oblation! May our transactions and the accruing gain be auspicious to us!

5. The wealth with which I go to purchase, desiring, ye gods, to gain wealth through wealth, may that grow more, not less! Drive away, O Agni, in return for the oblation, the gods who shut off gain!

6. The wealth with which I go to purchase, desiring, ye gods, to gain wealth through wealth, may Indra, Pragâpati, Savitar, Soma, Agni, place lustre into it for me!

7. We praise with reverence thee, O priest (Agni) Vaisvdnara. Do thou over our children, selves, cattle, and life's breath watch!

8. Daily, never failing, shall we bring (oblations to thee), O Gâtavedas, (as if fodder) to a horse standing (in the stable). In growth of wealth and nutriment rejoicing, may we, O Agni, thy neighbours, not take harm!

IV, 38. A. Prayer for success in gambling

1. The successful, victorious, skilfully gaming Apsarâ, that Apsarâ who makes the winnings in the game of dice, do I call hither.

2. The skilfully gaming Apsarâ who sweeps and heaps up (the stakes), that Apsarâ who takes the winnings in the game of dice, do I call hither.

May she, who dances about with the dice, when she takes the stakes from the game of dice, when she desires to win for us, obtain the advantage by (her) magic! May she come to us full of abundance! Let them not win this wealth of ours!

4. The (Apsarâs) who rejoice in dice, who carry grief and wrath-tbat joyful and exulting Apsarâ, do I call hither.

B. Prayer to secure the return of calves that have strayed to a distance

5. They (the cattle) who wander along the rays of the sun, or they who wander along the flood of light) they whose bull (the. sun), full of strength, from afar protecting, with the day wanders about all the worlds-may he (the bull), full of strength, delighting in this offering, come to us touether with the atmosphere!

6. Together with the atmosphere, O thou who art full of strength, protect the white (karkî) calf, O thou swift steed (the sun)! Here are many drops (of ghee) for thee; come hither! May this white calf (karkî) of thine, may thy mind, be here!

7. Together with the atmosphere, O thou who art full of strength, protect the white (karkî) calf, O thou swift steed (the sun)! Here is the fodder, here the stall, here do we tie down the calf. Whatever (are your) names, we own you. Hail!

VII, 50. Prayer for success at dice

1. As the lightning at all times smites irresistibly the tree, thus would I to-day irresistibly beat the gamesters with my dice!

2. Whether they be alert, or not alert, the fortune of (these) folks, unresisting, shall assemble from all sides, the gain (collect) within my hands!

3. I invoke with reverence Agni, who has his own riches; here attached he shall beap up gain for us! I procure (wealth) for myself, as if with chariots that win the race. May I accomplish auspiciously the song of praise to the Maruts!

4. May we by thy aid conquer the (adversary s) troop; help us (to obtain) our share in every contest! Make for us, O Indra, a good and ample road; crush, O Maghavan, the lusty power of our enemies!

5. I have conquered and cleaned thee out (?); I have also gained thy reserve. As the wolf plucks to pieces the sheep, thus do I pluck thy winnings.

6. Even the strong hand the bold player conquers, as the skilled gambler heaps up his winnings at the proper time. Upon him that loves the game

(the god), and does not spare his money, (the game, the god) verily bestows the delights of wealth.

7. Through (the possession of) cattle we all would suppress (our) wretched poverty, or with grain our hunger, O thou oft implored (god)! May we foremost among rulers, unharmed, gain wealth by our cunning devices!

8. Gain is deposited in my right hand, victory in my left. Let me become a conqueror of cattle, horses, wealth, and gold!

9. O dice, yield play, profitable as a cow that is rich in milk! Bind me to a streak of gain, as the bow (is bound) with the string!

VI, 56. Exorcism of serpents from the premises

1. May the serpent, ye gods, not slay us along with our children and our men! The closed (jaw) shall not snap open, the open one not close! Reverence (be) to the divine folk!

2. Reverence be to the black serpent, reverence to the one that is striped across! To the brown svaga reverence; reverence to the divine folk!

3. I clap thy teeth upon thy teeth, and also thy jaw upon thy jaw; I press thy tongue against thy tongue, and close up, O serpent, thy mouth.

X, 4. Charm against serpents, invoking the horse of Pedu that slays serpents

1. To Indra belongs the first chariot, to the gods the second chariot, to Varuna, forsooth, the third. The serpents' chariot is the last: it shall hit a post, and come to grief!

2. The young darbha-grass burns (the serpents?), the tail of the horse, the tail of the shaggy one, the seat of the wagon (burns the serpents?).

3. Strike down, O white (horse), with thy forefoot and thy hind-foot! As timber floating in water, the poison of the serpents, the fierce fluid, is devoid of strength.

4. Neighing loudly he dived down, and, again diving up, said: 'As timber floating in water, the poison of the serpents, the fierce fluid, is devoid of strength.'

5. The horse of Pedu slays the kasarnîla, the horse of Pedu slays the white (serpent), and also the black. The horse of Pedu cleaves the head of the ratharvî, the adder.

6. O horse of Pedu, go thou first: we come after thee! Thou shalt cast out the serpents from the road upon which we come!

7. Here the horse of Pedu was born; from here is his departure. Here are the tracks of the serpent-killing, powerful steed!

8. May the closed (serpent's jaw) not snap open, may the open one not close! The two serpents in this field, man and wife, they are both bereft of strength.

9. Without strength here are the serpents, those that are near, and those that are far. With a club do I slay the vriskika (scorpion), with a staff the serpent that has approached.

10. Here is the remedy for both the aghâsva and the svaga! Indra (and) Pedu's horse have put to naught the evil-planning (aghâyantam) serpent.

11. The horse of Pedu do we remember, the strong, with strong footing: behind he, staring forth, these adders.

12. Deprived are they of life's spirit, deprived of poison, slain by Indra with his bolt. Indra hath slain them: we have slain them.

13. Slain are they that are striped across, crushed are the adders! Slay thou the one that produces a hood, (slay) the white and the black in the darbha-grass!

14. The maiden of the Kirâta-tribe, the little one digs up the remedy, with golden spades, on the mountain's back.

15. Hither has come a youthful physician: he slays the speckled (serpent), is irresistible. He, forsooth, crushes the svaga and the vriskika both.

16. Indra did set at naught for me the serpent, (and so did) Mitra and Varuna, Vâta and Parganya both.

17. Indra did set at naught for me the serpent, the adder, male and female, the svaga, (the serpent) that is striped across, the kasarnîla, and the dasonasi.

18. Indra slew thy first ancestor, O serpent, and since they are crushed, what strength, forsooth, can be theirs?

19. I have gathered up their heads, as the fisherman the karvara (fish). I have gone off into the river's midst, and washed out the serpent's poison.

20. The poison of all serpents the rivers shall carry off! Slain are they that are striped across, crushed are the adders!

21. As skilfully I cull the fibre of the plants, as I guide the mares, (thus), O serpent, shall thy poison go away!

22. The poison that is in the fire, in the sun, in the earth, and in the plants, the kândâ-poison, the kanaknaka, thy poison shall go forth, and come!

23. The serpents that are sprung from the fire, that are sprung from the plants, that are sprung from the water, and originate from the lightning; they from whom great brood has sprung in many ways, those serpents do we revere with obeisance.

24. Thou art, (O plant), a maiden, Taudî by name.; Ghritâkî, forsooth, is thy name. Underfoot is thy place: I take in hand what destroys the poison.

25. From every limb make the poison start; shut it out from the heart! Now the force that is in thy poison shall go down below!

26. The poison has gone to a distance: he has shut it out; he has fused the poison with poison. Agni has put away the poison of the serpent, Soma has led it out. The poison has gone back to the biter. The serpent is dead!

XI, 2. Prayer to Bhava and Sarva for protection from dangers

1. O Bhava and Sarva, be merciful, do not attack (us); ye lords of beings, lords of cattle, reverence be to you twain! Discharge not your arrow even after it has been laid on (the bow), and has been drawn! Destroy not our bipeds and our quadrupeds!

2. Prepare not our bodies for the dog, or the jackal; for the aliklavas, the vultures, and the black birds! Thy greedy insects, O lord of cattle (pasu-pate), and thy birds shall not get us to devour!

3. Reverence we offer, O Bhava, to thy roaring, to thy breath, and to thy injurious qualities; reverence to thee, O Rudra, thousand-eyed, immortal!

4. We offer reverence to thee from the east, from the north, and from the - south; from (every) domain, and from heaven. Reverence be to thy atmosphere!

5. To thy face, O lord of cattle, to thy eyes, O Bhava, to thy skin, to thy form, thy appearance, (and to thy aspect) from behind, reverence be!

6. To thy limbs, to thy belly, to thy tongue, to thy mouth, to thy teeth, to thy smell (nose), reverence be!
7. May we not conflict with Rudra, the archer with the dark crest, the thousand-eyed, powerful one, the slayer of Ardhaka!

8. Bhava shall steer clear from us on all sides, Bhava shall steer clear from us, as fire from water! May he not bear malice towards us: reverence be to him!

9. Four times, eight times, be reverence to Bhava, ten times be reverence to thee, O lord of cattle! To thy (charge) have been assigned these five (kinds of) cattle: cows, horses, men, goats and sheep.

10. Thine, O strong god (ugra), are the four regions, thine the sky, thine the earth, and thine this broad atmosphere; thine is this all that has a spirit and has breath upon the earth.

11. Thine is this broad, treasure-holding receptacle within which all worlds are contained. Do thou spare us, O lord of cattle: reverence be to thee! Far from us shall go the jackals, evil omens, dogs; far shall go (the mourning women) who bewail rnisfortune with dishevelled hair!

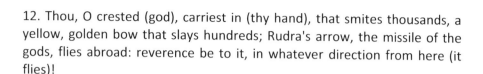

12. Thou, O crested (god), carriest in (thy hand), that smites thousands, a yellow, golden bow that slays hundreds; Rudra's arrow, the missile of the gods, flies abroad: reverence be to it, in whatever direction from here (it flies)!

13. The adversary who lurks and seeks to overcome thee, O Rudra, upon him thou dost fasten thyself from behind, as (the hunter) that follows the trail of a wounded (animal).

14. Bhava and Rudra, united and concordant, both strong (ugrau), ye advance to deeds of heroism: reverence be to both of them, in whatever direction (they are) from here!

15. Reverence be to thee coming, reverence to thee going; reverence, O Rudra, be to thee standing, and reverence, also, to thee sitting!

16. Reverence in the evening, reverence in the morning, reverence by night,reverence byday! I have offered reverence to Bhava and to Sarva, both.

17. Let us not with our tongue offend Rudra, who rushes on, thousand-eyed, overseeing all, who hurls (his shafts) forward, who is manifoldly wise!

18. We approach first the (god) that has dark horses, is black, sable, destructive, terrible, who casts down the car of Kesin: reverence be to him!

19. Do not hurl at us thy club, thy divine bolt; be not incensed at us, O lord of cattle! Shake over some other than us the celestial branch!

20. Injure us not, interpose for us, spare us, be not angry with us! Let us not contend with thee!
21. Do not covet our cattle, our men, our goats and sheep! Bend thy course elsewhere, O strong god (ugra), slay the offspring of the blasphemers!

22. He whose missile, fever and cough, assails the single (victim), as the snorting of a stallion, who snatches away (his victims) one by one, to him be reverence!

23. He who dwells fixed in the atmosphere, smiting the blasphemers of the god that do not sacrifice, to him be reverence with ten sakvarî-stanzas!

24. For thee the wild beasts of the forest have been placed in the forest: flamingoes, eagles, birds of prey, and fowls. Thy spirit, O lord of cattle, is within the waters, to strengthen thee the heavenly waters flow.

25. The dolphins, great serpents (boas), purîkayas (water-animals), sea-monsters, fishes, ragasas at which thou shootest-there exists for thee, O Bhava, no distance, and no barrier. At a glance thou lookest around the entire earth; from the eastern thou slayest in the northern ocean.

26. Do not, O Rudra, contaminate us with fever, or with poison, or with heavenly fire: cause this lightning to descend elsewhere than upon us!

27. Bhava rules the sky, Bhava rules the earth; Bhava has filled the broad: atmosphere. Reverence be to him in whatever direction from here (he abides)!

28. O king Bhava, be merciful to thy worshipper, for thou art the lord of living beasts! He who believes the gods exist, to his quadruped and biped be merciful!

29. Slay neither our great nor our small; neither those of us that are riding, nor those that shall ride; neither our father, nor our mother. Cause no injury, O Rudra, to our own persons!

30. To Rudra's howling dogs, who swallow their food without blessing, who have wide jaws, I have made this obeisance.

31. Reverence, O god, be to thy shouting hosts, reverence to thy long-haired, reverence to thy reverenced, reverence to thy devouring hosts! May well-being and security be to us!

IV, 28. Prayer to Bhava and Sarva for protection from calamities

1. O Bhava and Sarva, I am devoted to you. Take note of that, ye under whose control, is all this which shines (the visible universe)! Ye who rule all these two-footed and four-footed creatures, deliver us from calamity!

2. Ye to whom belongs all that is near by, yea, all that is far; ye who are known as the most skilful archers among bowmen; ye who rule all these two-footed and four-footed creatures, deliver us from calamity!

3. The thousand-eyed slayers of Vritra both do I invoke. I go praising the two strong gods (ugrau) whose pastures extend far. Ye who rule all these two-footed and four-footed creatures, deliver us from calamity!

4. Ye who, united, did undertake many (deeds) of old, and, moreover, did visit portents upon the. people; ye who rule all these two-footed and fourfooted creatures, deliver us from calamity!

5. Ye from whose blows no one either among gods or men escapes; ye who rule all these twofooted and four-footed creatures, deliver us from calamity!

6. The sorcerer who prepares a spell, or manipulates the roots (of plants) against us, against him, ye strong gods, launch your thunderbolt! Ye who rule all these two-footed and four-footed creatures, deliver us from calamity.

7. Ye strong gods, favour us in battles, bring into contact with your thunderbolt the Kimîdin! I praise you, O Bhava and Sarva, call fervently upon you in distress: deliver us from calamity!

VII, 9. Charm for finding lost property

1. On the distant path of the paths Pûshan was born, on the distant path of heaven, on the distant path of the earth. Upon the two most lovely places both he walks hither and away, knowing (the way).

2. Pûshan knows these regions all; he shall lead us by the most dangerless (way). Bestowing well-being, of radiant glow, keeping our heroes undiminished, he shall, alert and skilful, go before us!

3. O Pûshan, under thy law may we never suffer harm: as praisers of thee are we here!
4. Pûshan shall from the east place his right hand about us, shall bring again to us what has been lost: we shall come upon what has been lost!

VI, 128. Propitiation of the weather-prophet

1. When the stars made Sakadhûma their king they bestowed good weather upon him: 'This shall be his dominion,' they said.

2. Let us have good weather at noon, good weather at eve, good weather in the early morning, good weather in the niyht

3. For day and night, for the stars, for sun and moon, and for us prepare good weather, O king Sakadhûma!

4. To thee, O Sakadhûma, ruler of the stars, that gavest us good weather in the evening in the night, and by day, let there ever be obeisance!

XI, 6. Prayer for deliverance from calamity, addressed to the entire pantheon

1. To Agni we speak and to the trees, to the plants and to the herbs; to Indra, Brihaspati, and Sûya: they shall deliver us from calamity!

2. We speak to king Varuna, to Mitra, Vishnu and Bhaga. To Amsa and Vivasvant do we speak: they shall deliver us from calamity!

3. We speak to Savitar, the god, to Dhâtar, and to Pûshan; to first-born Tvashtar do we speak: they shall deliver us from calamity!

4. We speak to the Gandharvas and the Apsaras, to the Asvins and to Brahmanaspati, to the god whose name is Aryaman: they shall deliver us from calamity!

5. Now do we speak to day and night, to Sûrya (sun) and to Kandramas (moon), the twain; to all the Âdityas we speak: they shall deliver us from calamity!

6. We speak to Vâta (wind) and Parganya, to the atmosphere and the directions of space. And to all the regions do we speak: they shall deliver us from calamity!

7. Day and night, and Ushas (dawn), too, shall deliver thee from curses! Soma the god, whom they call Kandramas (moon), shall deliver me!

8. To the animals of the earth and those of heaven, to the wild beasts of the forest, to the winged birds, do we speak: they shall deliver us from calamity!

9. Now do we speak to Bhava and Sarva, to Rudra and Pasupati; their arrows do we know well: these (arrows) shall be ever propitious to us!

10. We speak to the heavens, and the stars, to earth, the Yakshas, and the mountains; to the seas.. the rivers, and the lakes: they shall deliver us from calamity!

11. To the seven Rishis now do we speak, to the divine waters and Pragâpati. To the Fathers with Yama at their head: they shall deliver us from calamity!

12. The gods that dwell in heaven, and those that dwell in the atmosphere; the mighty (gods) that are fixed upon the earth, they shall deliver us from

calamity!

13. The Âdityas, Rudras, Vasus, the divine Atharvans in heaven, and the wise Angiras: they shall deliver us from calamity!

14. We speak to the sacrifice and the sacrificer, to the riks, the sâmans, and the healing (Atharvan) charms; we speak to the yagus-formulas and the invocations (to the gods): they shall deliver us from calamity!

15. We speak to the five kingdoms of the plants with soma the most excellent among them. The darbha-grass, hemp, and mighty barley: they shall deliver us from calamity!

16. We speak to the Arâyas (demons of grudge), Rakshas, serpents, pious men, and Fathers; to the one and a hundred deaths: they shall deliver us from calamity!

17. To the seasons we speak, to the lords of the seasons, and to the sections of the year; to the halfyears, years, and months: they shall deliver us from calamity!

18. Come, ye gods, from the south and the west; ye gods in the east come forth! From the east, from the north the mighty gods, all the gods assembled: they shall deliver us from calamity!

19, 20. We speak here to all the gods that hold to their agreements, promote the order (of the universe), together with all their wives: they shall deliver us from calamity!

21. We speak to being, to the lord of being, and also to him that controls the beings; to the beings all assembled: they shall deliver us from calamity!

22. The five divine regions, the twelve divine seasons, the teeth of the year, they shall ever be propitious, to us!

23. The amrita (ambrosia), bought for the price of a chariot, which Mâtalî knows as a remedy, that Indra stored away in the waters: that, O ye waters, furnish ye as a remedy!

CHARMS IN EXPIATION OF SIN AND DEFILEMENT

VI, 45. Prayer against mental delinquency

1. Pass far away, O sin of the mind! Why dost thou utter things not to be uttered? Pass away, I love thee not! To the trees, the forests go on! With the house, the cattle, is my mind.

2. What wrongs we have committed through imprecation, calumny, and false speech, either awake, or asleep--Agni shall put far away from us all offensive evil deeds!

3. What, O Indra Brahmanaspati, we do falselymay Praketas ('care-taker') Ângirasa protect us from misfortune, and from evil!

VI, 26. Charm to avert evil

1. Let me go, O evil; being powerful, take thou pity on us! Set me, O evil, unharmed, into the world of happiness!

2. If, O evil, thou dost not abandon us, then do we abandon thee at the fork of the road. May evil follow after another (man)!

3. Away from us may thousand-eyed, immortal (evil) dwell! Him whom we hate may it strike, and him whom we hate do thou surely smite!

VI, 114. Expiatory formula for imperfections in the sacrifice

1. The god-angering (deed), O ye gods, that we, the (Brahman) gods, have committed, from that do ye, O Âdityas, release us, by virtue of the order of the universe!

2. By virtue of the order of the universe do ye, O reverend Âdityas, release us here, if, O ye carriers of the sacrifice, though desirous of accomplishing (the sacrifice), we did not accomplish (it)!--

3. (If), when sacrificing with the fat (animal), when offering oblations of ghee with the spoon, when desiring to benefit you, O all ye gods, we have contrary to desire, not succeeded!

VI, 115. Expiatory formulas for sins

1. From the sins which knowingly or unknowingly we have committed, do ye, all gods, of one accord, release us!

2. If awake, or if asleep, to sin inclined, I have committed a sin, may what has been, and what shall be, as if from a wooden post, release me!

3. As one released from a wooden post, as one in a sweat by bathing (is cleansed) of filth, as ghee is clarified by the sieve, may all (the gods) clear me from sin!

VI, 112. Expiation for the precedence of a younger brother over an older

1. May this (younger brother) not slay the oldest one of them, O Agni; protect him that he be not torn out by the root! Do thou here cunningly loosen the fetter of Grâhi (attack of disease); may all the gods give thee leave!

2. Free these three, O Agni, from the three fetters with which they have been shackled! Do thou cunningly loosen the fetters of Grâhi; release them all, father, sons, and mother!

3. The fetters with which the older brother, whose younger brother has married before him, has been bound, with which he has been encumbered and shackled limb by limb, may they be loosened; since fit for loosening they are! Wipe off, O Pûshan, the misdeeds upon him that practiseth abortion!

VI, 113. Expiation for certain heinous crimes

1. On Trita the gods wiped off this sin, Trita wiped it off on human beings; hence if Grâhi (attack of disease) has seized thee, may these gods remove her by means of their charm!

2. Enter into the rays, into smoke, O sin; go into the vapours, and into the fog! Lose thyself on the foam of the river! 'Wipet off, O Pûshan, the misdeeds upon him that practiseth abortion!

3. Deposited in twelve places is that which has been wiped off Trita, the sins belonging to humanity. Hence if Grâhi has seized thee, may these gods remove her by means of their charm!

VI, 120. Prayer for heaven after remission of sins

1. If air, or earth and heaven, if mother or father, we have injured, may this Agni Gârhapatya (household fire) without fail lead us out from this (crime)

to the world of well-doing!
2. The earth is our mother, Aditi (the universe) our kin, the air our protector from hostile schemes. May father sky bring prosperity to us from the world of the Fathers; may I come to my (departed) kin, and not lose heaven!

3. In that bright world where our pious friends live in joy, having cast aside the ailments of their own bodies, free from lameness, not deformed in limb, there may we behold our parents and our children!

VI, 27. Charm against pigeons regarded as ominous birds

1. O ye gods, if the pigeon, despatched as the messenger of Nirriti (the goddess of destruction), hath come here seeking (us out), we shall sing his praises, and prepare (our) ransom. May our two-footed and four-footed creatures be prosperous!

2. Auspicious to us shall be the pigeon that has been despatched; harmless, ye gods, the bird shall be to our house! The sage Agni shall verily take pleasure in our oblation; the winged missile shall avoid us!

3. The winged missile shall not do us injury: upon our hearth, our fireplace he (the pigeon) takes his steps! Propitious he shall be to our cattle and

our domestics; may not, ye gods, the pigeon here do harm to us!

VI, 29. Charm against ominous pigeons and owls

1. Upon those persons yonder the winged missile shall fall! If the owl shrieks, futile shall this be, or if the pigeon takes his steps upon the fire!

2. To thy two messengers, O Nirriti, who come here, despatched or not despatched, to our house, to the pigeon and to the owl, this shall be no place to step upon!

3. He shall not fly hither to slaughter (our) men; to keep (our) men sound he shall settle here! Charm .him very far away unto a distant region, that (people) shall behold you (i.e. him) in Yama's house devoid of strength, that they shall behold you bereft of power!

VII, 64. Expiation when one is defiled by a black bird of omen

1. What this black bird flying forth towards (me) has dropped here--may the waters protect me from all that misfortune and evil!

2. What this black bird has brushed here with thy mouth, O Nirtiti (goddess of misfortune)-may Agni Gârhapatya (the god of the household fire) free me from this sin!

VI, 46. Exorcism of evil dreams

1. Thou who art neither alive nor dead, the immortal child of the gods art thou, O Sleep! Varunânî is thy mother, Yama (death) thy father, Araru is thy name.

2. We know, O Sleep, thy birth, thou art the son of the divine women-folk, the instrument of Yama (death)! Thou art the ender, thou art death! Thus do we know thee, O Sleep: do thou, O Sleep, protect us from evil dreams!

3. As one pays off a sixteenth, an eighth, or an (entire) debt, thus do we transfer every evil dream upon our enemy.

VII, 115. Charm for the removal of evil characteristics, and the acquisition of auspicious ones

1. Fly forth from here, O evil mark, vanish from here, fly forth to yonder place! Upon him that hates us do we fasten thee with a brazen hook.

2. The unsavoury mark which flying has alighted upon me, as a creeper upon a tree, that mayest thou put away from us, away from here, O golden-handed

(golden-rayed) Savitar (the sun), bestowing goods upon us!
3. Together with the body of the mortal, from his birth, one and a hundred marks are born. Those that are most foul do we drive away from here; the auspicious ones, O Gâtavedas (Agni), do thou hold fast for us!

4. These (marks) here I have separated, as cows scattered upon the heather. The pure marks shall remain, the foul ones I have made to disappear!

PRAYERS AND IMPRECATIONS IN THE INTEREST OF THE BRAHMANS

V, 18. Imprecation against the oppressors of Brahmans

1. The gods, O king, did not give to thee this (Cow) to eat. Do not, O prince, seek to devour the cow of the Brâhmana, which is unfit to be eaten!

2. The prince, beguiled by dice, the wretched one who has lost as a stake his own person, he may, perchance, eat the cow of the Brâhmana, (thinking), 'let me live to-day (if) not to-morrow'!

3. Enveloped (is she) in her skin, as an adder with evil poison; do not, O prince, (eat the cow) of the Brâhmana: sapless, unfit to be eaten, is that cow!

4. Away does (the Brâhmana) take regal power, destroys vigour; like fire which has caught does he burn away everything. He that regards the Brâhmana as fit food drinks of the poison of the taimâta-serpent.

5. He who thinks him (the Brahman) mild, and slays him, he who reviles the gods, lusts after wealth, without thought, in his heart Indra kindles a fire; him both heaven and earth hate while he lives.

6. The Brâhmana must not be encroached upon, any more than fire, by him that regards his own body! For Soma is his (the Brâhmana's) heir, Indra protects him from hostile plots.

7. He swallows her (the cow), bristling with a hundred hooks, (but) is unable to digest her, he, the fool who, devouring the food of the Brahmans, thinks, 'I am eating a luscious (morsel).'

8. (The Brahman's) tongue turns into a bow. string, his voice into the neck of an arrow; his windpipe, his teeth are bedaubed with holy fire: with these the Brahman strikes those who revile the gods, by means of bows that have the strength to reach the heart, discharged by the gods.

9. The Brâhmanas have sharp arrows, are armed with missiles, the arrow whi ch they hurl goes not in vain; pursuing him with their holy fire and their wrath, even from afar, do they pierce him.

10. They who ruled over a thousand, and were themselves ten hundred, the Vaitahavya, when they devoured the cow of the Brâhmana, perished.

11. The cow herself, when slaughtered, came down upon the Vaitahavyas. who had roasted for themselves the last she-goat of Kesaraprâbandhâ.

12. The one hundred and one persons whom the earth did cast off, because they had injured the offspring of a Brâhmana, were ruined irretrievably.

13. As a reviler of the gods does he live among mortals, having swallowed poison, he becomes more bone (than flesh). He that injureth a Brâhmana, whose kin are the gods, does not reach heaven by the road of the Fathers.

14. Agni is called our guide, Soma our heir, Indra slays those who curse (us): that the strong (sages) know.

15. Like a poisoned arrow, O king, like -an adder, O lord of cattle, is the terrible arrow of the Brâhmana: with that he smites those who revile (the gods).

V, 19. Imprecation against the oppressors of Brahmans

1. Beyond measure they waxed strong, just fell short of touching the heavens. When they infringed upon Bhrigu they perished, the Sriñgaya Vaitahavyas.

2. The persons who pierced Brihatsâman, the descendant of Angiras, the Brâhmana--a ram with two rows of teeth, a sheep devoured their offspring.

3. They who spat upon the Brâhmana, who desired tribute from him, they sit in the middle of a pool of blood, chewing hair.

4. The cow of the Brahman, when roasted, as far as she reaches does she destroy the lustre of the kingdom; no lusty hero is born (there).

5. A cruel (sacrilegious) deed is her slaughter, her meat, when eaten, is sapless; when her milk is drunk, that surely is accounted a crime against the Fathers.

6. When the king, weening himself mighty, desires to destroy the Brâhmana, then royal power is dissipated, where the Brâhmana is oppressed.

7. Becoming eight-footed, four-eyed, four-eared, four-jawed, two-mouthed, two-tongued, she dispels the rule of the oppressor of the Brahman.

8. That (kingdom) surely she swamps, as water a leaking ship; misfortune strikes that kingdom, in which they injure a Brâhmana.

9. The trees chase away with the words: 'do not come within our shade,' him who covets the wealth that belongs to a Brâhmana, O Nârada!

10. King Varuna pronounced this (to be) poison, prepared by the gods: no one who has devoured the cow of a Brâhmana retains the charge of a kingdom.

11. Those full nine and ninety whom the earth did cast off, because they had injured the offspring of a Brâhmana, were ruined irretrievably.

12. The kûdî-plant (Christ's thorn) that wipes away the track (of death), which they fasten to the dead, that very one, O oppressor of Brahmans, the gods did declare (to be) thy couch.

13. The tears which have rolled from (the eyes of) the oppressed (Brahman), as he laments, these very ones, O oppressor of Brahmans, the gods did assign to thee as thy share of water.

14. The water with which they bathe the dead, with which they moisten his beard, that very one, O oppressor of Brahmans, the gods did assign to thee as thy share of water.

15. The rain of Mitra and Varuna does not moisten the oppressor of Brahmans; the assembly is not complacent for him, he does not guide his friend according to his will.

V, 7. Prayer to appease Arâti, the demon of grudge and avarice

1. Bring (wealth) to us, do not stand in our way, O Arâti; do not keep from us the sacrificial reward as it is being taken (to us)! Adoration be to the power of grudge, the power of failure, adoration to Arâti!

2. To thy advising minister, whom thou, Arâti, didst make thy agent, do we make obeisance. Do not bring failure to my wish!

3. May our wish, instilled by the gods, be fulfilled by day and night! We go in quest of Arâti. Adoration be to Arâti!

4. Sarasvatî (speech), Anumati (favour), and Bhaga (fortune) we go to invoke. Pleasant, honied, words I have spoken on the occasions when the gods were invoked.

5. Him whom I implore with Vâk Sarasvatî (the goddess-of speech), the yoke-fellow of thought, faith shall find to-day, bestowed by the brown soma!

6. Neither our wish nor our speech do thou frustrate! May Indra and Agni both bring us wealth! Do ye all who to-day desire to make gifts to us gain favour with Arâti!

7. Go far away, failure! Thy missile do we avert. I know thee (to be) oppressive and piercing, O Arâti!
8. Thou dost even transform thyself into a naked woman, and attach thyself to people in their sleep, frustrating, O Arâti, the thought, and intention of man.

9. To her who, great, and of great dimension, did penetrate all the regions, to this golden-locked Nirriti (goddess of misfortune), I have rendered obeisance.

10. To the gold-complexioned, lovely one, who rests upon golden cushions, to the great one, to that Arâti who wears golden robes, I have rendered obeisance.

XII, 4. The necessity of giving away sterile cows to the Brahmans

1. 'I give,' he shall surely say,'the sterile cow to the begging Brahmans'--and they have noted her--that brings progeny and offspring!

2. With his offspring does he trade, of his cattle is he deprived, that refuses to give the cow of the gods to the begging descendants of the Rishis.

3. Through (the gift of) a cow with broken horns his (cattle) breaks down, through a lame one he tumbles into a pit, through a mutilated one his house is burned, through a one-eyed one his property is given away.

4. Flow of blood attacks the cattle-owner from the spot where her dung is deposited: this understanding there is about the vasâ (the sterile cow); for thou (sterile cow) art said to be very difficult to deceive!

5. From the resting-place of her feet the (disease) called viklindu overtakes (the owner, or the cattle). Without sickness breaks down (the cattle) which she sniffs upon with her nose.

6. He that pierces her ears is estranged from the gods. He thinks: 'I am making a mark (upon her),' (but) he diminishes his own property.

7. If any one for whatsoever purpose cuts her tail then do his colts die, and the wolf tears his calves.
8. If a crow has injured her hair, as long as she is with her owner then do his children die: decline overtakes them without (noticeable) sickness.

9. If the serving-maid sweeps together her dung, that bites as lye, there arises from this sin disfigurement that passeth not away.

10. The sterile cow in her very birth is born for the gods and Brâhmanas. Hence to the Brahmans she is to be given: that, they say, guarantees the security of one's own property.

11. For those that come requesting her the cow has been created by the gods. Oppression of Brahmans it is called, if he keeps her for himself.

12. He that refuses to give the cow of the gods to the descendants of the Rishis who ask for it, infringes upon the gods, and the wrath of the Brâhmanas.

13. Though he derives benefit from this sterile cow, another (cow) then shall he seek! When kept she injures (his) folk, if he refuses to give her after she has been asked for!

14. The sterile cow is as a treasure deposited for die Brâhmanas: they come here for her, with whomsoever she is born.

15. The Brâhmanas come here for their own, when they come for the sterile cow. The refusal of her is, as though he were oppressing them in other concerns.

I& If she herds up to her third year, and no disease is discovered in her, and he finds her to be a sterile cow, O Nârada, then must he look for the Brâhmanas.

17. If he denies that she is sterile, a treasure deposited for the gods, then Bhava and Sarva, both, come upon him, and hurl their arrow upon him.

18. Though he does not perceive upon her either udder, or tits, yet both yield him milk, if he has prevailed upon himself to give away the sterile cow.

19. Hard to cheat, she oppresses him, if, when asked for, he refuses to give her. His desires are not fulfilled, if he aims to accomplish them without giving her away.

20. The gods did ask for the sterile cow, making the Brâhmana their mouthpiece. The man that does not give (her) enters into the wrath of all of these.

21. Into the wrath of the cattle enters he that gives not the sterile cow to the Brâhmanas; if he, the mortal, appropriates the share deposited for the gods.

22. Even if a hundred other Brâhmanas beg the owner for the sterile cow, yet the gods did say anent her: 'The cow belongs to him that knoweth thus.'

23. He that refuses the sterile cow to him that knoweth thus, and gives her to others, difficult to dwell upon is for him the earth with her divinities.

24. The gods did beg the sterile cow of him wilh whom she was born at first. That very one Nârada recognised and drove forth in company with the gods.

25. The sterile cow renders childless, and poor in cattle, him that yet appropriates her, when she has been begged for by the Brâhmanas.

26. For Agni and Soma, for Kâma, for Mitra, and for Varuna, for these do the Brâhmanas beg her: upon these he infringes, if he gl ves her not.

27. As long as the owner does not himself hear the stanzas referring to (the giving away of) her, she may herd among his cattle; (only) if he has not heard (them) may she pass the night in his house.

28. He that has listened to the stanzas, yet has permitted her to herd among the cattle, his life and prosperity the angry gods destroy.

29. The sterile cow, even when she rambles freely, is a treasure deposited for the gods. Make evident thy true nature when thou desirest to go to thy (proper) stable!

30. She makes evident her nature when she desires to go to her (proper) stable. Then indeed the sterile cow puts it into the minds of the Brahmans to beg (for her).

31. She evolves it in her mind, that (thought) reaches the gods. Then do the Brahmans come to beg for the sterile cow.

32. The call svadhâ befriends him with the Fathers, the sacrifice with the gods. Through the gift of the sterile cow the man of royal caste incurs not the anger of (her), his mother.

33. The sterile cow is the mother of the man of royal caste: thus was it from the beginning. It is said to be no (real) deprivation if she is given to the Brahmans.

34. As if he were to rob the ghee ladled up for Agni (the fire) from the (very) spoon, thus, if he gives not the sterile cow to the Brahmans, does he infringe upon Agni.

35. The sterile cow has the purodasa (sacrificial cake) for her calf, she yields plentiful milk, helps in this world, and fulfils all wishes for him that gives her (to the Brahmans).

36. The sterile cow fulfils all wishes in the kingdom of Yama for him that gives her. But they say that hell falls to the lot of him that withholds her, when she has been begged for.

37. The sterile cow, even if she should become fruitful, lives in anger at her owner: 'since he did regard me as sterile (without giving me to the Brahmans), he shall be bound in the fetters of death!'

38, He who thinks that the cow is sterile, and (yet) roasts her at home, even his children qnd grandchildren Brihaspati causes to be importuned (for her).

39. Fiercely does the (supposed) sterile cow burn when she herds with the cattle, though she be a (fruitful) cow. She verily, too, milks poison for the owner that does not present her.

40. It pleases the cattle when she is given to the Brahmans; moreover, the sterile cow is pleased, when she is made an offering to the gods (Brahmans).

41. From the sterile cows which the gods, returning from the sacrifice, created, Nârada picked out as (most) terrible the viliptî.

42. In reference to her the gods reflected: 'Is she a sterile cow, or not?' And Nârada in reference to her said: 'Of sterile cows she is the most sterile!'

43. 'How many sterile cows (are there), O Nârada, which thou knowest to be born among men?' About these do I ask thee, that knowest: 'Of which may the non-Brâhmana not eat?'

44. Of the viliptî, of her that has born a sterile cow, and of the sterile cow (herself), the non-Brâhmana, that hopes for prosperity, shall not eat!

45. Reverence be to thee, O Nârada, that knowest thoroughly which sterile cow is the most terrible, by withholding which (from the Brahmans) destruction is.incurred.

46. The viliptî, O Brihaspati, her that has, begotten a sterile cow, and the sterile cow (herself), the non-Brâhmana, that hopes for prosperity, shall not eat!

47. Three kinds, forsooth, of sterile cows are there: the viliptî, she that has begotten a sterile cow, and the sterile cow (herself). These he shall give to the Brahmans; (then) does he not estrange himself from Pragâpati.

48. 'This is your oblation, O Brâhmanas,' thus shall he reflect, if he is supplicated, if they ask him for the sterile cow, terrible in the house of him that refuses to give her.

49. The gods animadverted in reference to Bheda and the sterile cow, angry because he had not given her, in these verses-and therefore he (Bheda) perished.

50. Bheda did not present the sterile cow, though requested by Indra: for this sin the gods crushed him in battle.

51. The counsellors that advise the withholding (of the sterile cow), they, the rogues, in their folly, conflict with the wrath of Indra.

52. They who lead the owner of cattle aside, then say to him: 'do not give,' in their folly they run into the missile hurled by Rudra.

53. And if he roasts the sterile cow at home, whether he makes a sacrifice of her, or not, he sins against the gods and Brâhmanas, and as a cheat falls from heaven.

XI, 1. The preparation of the brahmaudana, the porridge given as a fee to the Brahmans

1. O Agni, come into being! Aditi here in her throes, longing for sons, is cooking the porridge for the Brahmans, The seven Rishis, that did create the beings, shall here churn thee, along with progeny!

2. Produce the smoke, ye lusty friends; unharmed by wiles go ye into the contest! Here is the Agni (fire) who gains battles, and commands powerful warriors, with whom the gods did conquer the demons.

3. O Agni, to a great heroic deed thou wast aroused, to cook the Brahman's porridge, O Gâtavedas! The seven Rishis, that did create the beings, have produced thee. Grant her (the wife) wealth together with undiminished heroes!

4. Burn, O Agni, after having been kindled by the firewood, bring skilfully hither the gods that are to be revered! Causing the oblation to cook for these (Brahmans), do thou raise this (sacrificer) to the highest firmament!

5. The, threefold share which was of yore assigned to you (belongs) to the gods, the (departed) Fathers, and to the mortals (the priests). Know your shares! I divide them for you: the (share) of the gods shall protect this (woman)!

6. O Agni, possessed of might, superior, thou dost without fail prevail! Bend down to the ground our hateful rivals!--This measure, that is being measured, and has been measured, may constitute thy kin into (people) that render thee tribute!

7. Mayest thou together with thy kin be endowed with sap! Elevate her (the wife) to great heroism! Ascend on high to the base of the firmament, which they call 'the world of brightness'!

8. This great goddess earth, kindly disposed, shall receive the (sacrificial) skin! Then may we go to the world of well-doing (heaven)!

9. Lay these two press-stones, well coupled, upon the skin; crush skilfully the (soma-) shoots for the sacrificer! Crush down, (O earth), and beat down, those who are hostile to her (the wife); lift up high, and elevate her offspring!

10. Take into thy hands, O man, the press-stones that work together: the gods that are to be revered have come to thy sacrifice! Whatever three wishes thou dost choose, I shall here procure for thee unto fulfilment.

11. This, (O winnowing-basket), is thy purpose, and this thy nature: may Aditi, mother of heroes, take hold of thee! Winnow out those who are hostile to this (woman); afford her wealth and undiminished heroes!

12. Do ye, (O grains), remain in the (winnowing-) basket, while (the wind) blows over you; be separated, ye who are fit for the sacrifice, from the chaff! May we in happiness be superior to all our equals! I bend down under our feet those that hate us.

13. Retire, O woman, and return promptly! The stable of the waters (water-vessel) has settled upon thee, that thou mayest carry it: of these (the waters) thou shalt take such as are fit for sacrifice; having intelligently divided them off, thou shalt leave the rest behind!

14. These bright women, (the waters), have come hither. Arise, thou woman, and gather strength! To thee, that art rendered by thy husband a true wife, (and) by thy children rich in offspring, the sacrifice has come: receive the (water-) vessel!

15. The share of food that belongs to you of yore has been set aside for you. Instructed by the Rishis bring thou (woman) hither this water! May this sacrifice win advancement for you, win prAection, win offspring for you; may it be mighty, win cattle, and heroes for you!

16. O Agni, the sacrificial pot has settled upon thee: do thou shining, brightly glowing, heat it with thy glow! May the divine descendants of the Rishis, assembled about their share (of the porridge), full of fervour, heat this (pot) at the proper time!

17. Pure and clear may these sacrificial women, the waters bright, flow into the pot! The), have given us abundant offspring and cattle. May he that cooks the porridge go to the world of the pious (heaven)!

18. Purified by (our) prayer, and clarified by the ghee are the soma-shoots, (and) these sacrificial grains. Enter the water; may the pot receive you! When ye have cookect this (porridge) go ye to the world of the pious (heaven)!

19. Spread out far unto great extent, with a thousand surfaces, in the world of the pious! Grandfathers, fathers, children, grandchildren--I am the fifteenth one that did cook thee.

20. The porridge has a thousand surfaces, a hundred streams, and is indestructible; it is the road of the gods, leads to heaven. Yonder (enemies) do I place upon thee: injure them and their offspring; (but) to me that brings gifts thou shalt be merciful!

21. Step upon the altar (vedi); make this woman thrive in her progeny; repel the demons.; advance her! May we in happiness be superior to all our equals! I bend down under our feet all those that hate us.

22. Turn towards her with cattle, (thou pot), face towards her, together with the divine powers! Neither curses nor hostile magic shall reach thee; rule in thy dwelling free from disease!

23. Properly built, placed with care, this altar (vedi) has been arranged of yore for the Brahmans porridge. Put it, O woman, upon the purified amsadhrl; place there the porridge for the divine (Brâhmanas)!

24. May this sacrificial ladle (sruk), the second hand of Aditi, which the seven Rishis, the creators of the beings, did fashion, may this spoon, knowing the limbs of the porridge, heap it upon the altar!

25. The divine (Brâhmanas) shall sit down to thee, the cooked saerfice: do thou again descending from the fire, approach them! Clarified by soma settle in the belly of the Brâhmanas; the descendants of the Rishis who eat thee shall not take harm!

26. O king Soma, infuse harmony into the good Brâhmanas who shall sit about thee! Eagerly do I invite to the porridge the Rishis, descended from Rishis, that are born of religious fervour, and gladly obey the call.

27. These pure and clear sacrificial women (the waters) I put into the hands of the Brâhmanas severally. With whatever wish I pour this upon you, may Indra. accompanied by the Maruts grant this to me!

28. This gold is my immortal light, this ripe fruit of the field is my wish-granting cow. This treasure I present to the Brâhmanas: I prepare for myself a road that leads. to the Fathers in the heavens.

29. Scatter the spelt into Agni Gâtavedas (the fire), sweep away to a far distance the chaff! This (chaff) we have heard, is the share of the ruler of the house (Agni), and we know, too, what belonos to Nirriti (destruction) as her share.

30. Note, (O porridge), him that takes pains, and cooks and presses the soma; lift him up to the heavenly road, upon which, after he has reached the fullest age, he shall ascend to the highest firmament, the supreme heavens!

31. Anoint (with ghee), O adhvaryu (priest), the surface of this sustaining (porridge), make skilfully a place for the melted butter; with ghee do thou anoint all its limbs! I prepare for myself a road that leads to the Fathers in the heavens.

32. O sustaining (porridge), cast destruction and strife among such as are sitting about thee, and are not Brâhmanas! (But) the descendants of the - Rishis, that eat thee, being full of substance, spreading forth, shall not take harm!

33. To the descendants of the Rishis I make thee over, O porridge; those who are not descended from Rishis have no share in it! May Agni as my guardian, may all the Maruts, and all the gods watch over the cooked food!

34. Thee (the porridge) that milkest the sacrifice, art evermore abundant, the male milch-cow, the seat of wealth, we beseech for immortality of off-spring and long life with abundance of wealth.

35. Thou art a lusty male, penetratest heaven: go thou to the Rishis, descended from Rishis! Dwell in the world of the pious: there is a well-prepared (place) for us two!

36. Pack thyself up, go forth! O Agni, prepare the roads, that lead to the gods! By these: well-prepared (roads) may we reach the sacrifice, standing upon the firmament (that shines) with seven rays!

37. With the light with which the gods, having cooked the porridge for the Brâmanas, ascended to heaven, to the world of the pious, with that would we go to the world of the pious, ascending to the light, to the highest firmament!

XII, 3. The preparation of the brahmaudana, the porridge given as a fee to the Brahmans

1. (Thyself) a male, step thou upon the hide of the male (steer): go, call thither all that is dear to thee! At whatever age ye two formerly did first unite (in marriage), may that age be your common lot in Yama's kingdom!

2. Your sight shall be as clear (as formerly), your strength as abundant, your lustre as great, your vitality as manifold! When Agni, the (funeral-) pyre, fastens himself upon the corpse, then as a pair ye.shall rise from the (cooked) porridge!

3. Come ye together in this world, upon the road to the gods, and in Yama's realms! By purifications purified call ye together the offspring that has sprung from you!

4. Around the water united, sit ye down, O children; around this living (father) and the waters that refresh the living! Partake of these (waters), and of that porridge which the mother of you two cooks, and which is called amrita (ambrosia)!

5. The porridge which the father of you two, and which the mother cooks, unto freedom from defilement and foulness of speech, that porridge with a hundred streams (of ghee), leading to heaven, has penetrated with might both the hemispheres of the world.

6. In that one of the two hemispheres and the two heavenly worlds, conquered by the pious, which especially abounds in light, and is rich in honey, in that do ye in the fulness of time come together with your children!

7. Keep ever on in an easterly direction: this is the region that the faithful cling to! When your cooked porridge has been prepared on the fire, hold together, O man and wife, that ye may guard it!

8. When ye shall have reached the southerly direction, turn ye to this vessel! In that Yama, associated with the fathers, shall give abundant protection to your cooked porridge!

9. This westerly direction is especially favoured: in it Soma is ruler and consoler. To this hold, attach yourselves to the pious: then as a pair ye shall rise from the cooked porridge!

10. The northerly direction shall make our realm the very uppermost, in offspring, uppermost! The purusha is the metre pahkti: with all (our kin), endowed with all their limbs, may we be united!

11. This 'firm' direction (nadir) is Virâg (brilliancy): reverence be to her; may she be kind to my children and to me! Mayest thou, O goddess Aditi, who boldest all treasures, as an alert guardian guard the cooked porridge!

12. As a father his children do thou, (O earth), embrace us; may gentle winds blow upon us here on earth! Then the porridge which the two divinities (the sacrificer and his wife) are here preparing for us shall take note of our religious fer~our and our truth!

13. Whatever the black bird, that has come hither stealthily, has touched of that ahich has stuck to the rim, or whatever the wet-banded slavegirl does pollute-may ye, O waters, purify (that) mortar and pestle!

14. May this sturdy press-stone, with broad bottom, purified by the purifiers, beat away the Rakshas! Settle upon the skin, afford firm protection; may man and wife not come to grief in their children!

15. The (pestle of) wood has come to us together with the gods: it drives away the Rakshas and Pisâkas. Up it shall rise, shall let its voice resound

through it let us conquer all the worlds!
16. The cattle clothed itself in sevenfold strength, those among them that are sleek and those that are poor. The thirty-three gods attend them mayest thou, (O cattle), guide us to the heavenly world!

17. To the bright world of heaven thou shalt lead us; (there) let us be united with wife and children! I take her hand, may she follow me there; neither Nirriti (destruction), nor Arâti (grudge), shall gain mastery over us!

18. May we get past the evil Grâhi (seizure)! Casting aside darkness do thou, (O pestle), let thy lovely voice resound; do not, O wooden tool, when raised, do injury; do not mutilate the grain devoted to the gods!

19. All-embracing, about to be covered with ghee, enter, (O pot), as a co-dweller this space!--Take hold of the winnowing-basket, that has been grown by the rain: the spelt and the chaff it shall sift out!

20. Three regions are constructed after the pattern of the Brâhmana: yonder heaven, the earth, and the atmosphere.--Take the (soma-) shoots, and hold one another, (O man and wife)! They (the shoots) shall swell (with moisture), and again go back into the winnowing-basket!

21. Of manifold variegated colours are the animals, one colour hast thou, (O porridge), when successfully prepared.--Push these (soma-) Shoots upon this red skin; the press-stone shall purify them as the washer-man his clothes!

22. Thee, the (pot of) earth, I place upon the earth: your substance is the same, though thine, (O pot), is modified. Even though a blow has cracked or scratched thee, do not therefore burst: with this verse do I cover that up!

23. Gently as a mother embrace the son: I unite thee, (pot of) earth, with the earth! Mayest thou, the hollow pot, not totter upon the altar, when thou art pressed by the tools of sacrifice and the ghee!

24. May Agni who cooks thee protect thee on the east, Indra with the Maruts protect thee on the south! May Varuna on the west support thee upon thy foundation, may Soma on the north hold thee together!

25. Purified by the purifiers, the (waters) flow pure from the clouds, they reach to the spaces of heaven, and of the earth. They are alive, refresh the livino, and are firmly rooted: may Agni heat them, after they have been poured into the vessel!

26. From heaven they come, into the earth they penetrate; from the earth they penetrate into the atmosphere. May they, now pure, yet purify themselves further; may they conduct us to the heavenly world!

27. Whether ye are over-abundant or just sufficient, ye are surely clear, pure, and immortal: cook, ye waters, instructed by the husband and wife, obliging and helpful, the porridge!

28. Counted drops penetrate into the earth, commensurate with the breaths of life and the plants. The uncounted golden (drops), that are poured into (the porridge), have, (themselves) pure, established complete purity.

29. The boiling waters rise and sputter, cast up foam and many bubbles. Unite, ye waters, with this grain, as a woman who beholds her husband in the proper season!

30. Stir up (the grains) as they settle at the bottom: let them mingle their inmost parts with the waters! The water here I have measured with cups; measured was the grain, so as to be according to these regulations.

31. Hand over the sickle, with haste bring promptly (the grass for the barhis); without giving pain let them cut the plants at the joints! They whose kingdom Soma rules, the plants, shall not harbour anger against us!

32. Strew a new barhis for the porridge: pleasing to its heart, and lovely to its sight it shall be! Upon it the gods together with the goddesses shall enter; settle down to this (porridge) in proper order, and eat it!

33. O (instrument of) wood, settle down upon the strewn barhis, in keeping with the divinities and the agnishloma rites! Well shaped, as if by a carpenter (Tvashtar) with his axe, is thy form. Longing for this (porridge) the (gods) shall be seen about the vessel!

34. In sixty autumns the treasurer (of the porridge) shall fetch it, by the cooked grain he shall obtain heaven; the parents and the children shall live upon it. Bring thou this (man) to heaven, into the presence of Agni!

35. (Thyself) a holder, (O pot), hold on to the foundation of the earth: thee, that art immoveable the gods (alone) shall move! Man and wife, alive, with living children, shall remove thee from the hearth of the fire!

36. Thou hast conquered and reached all worlds; as many as are our wishes, thou hast satisfied them. Dip ye in, stirring stick and spoon! Place it (the por idge) upon a single dish!

37. Lay (ghee) upon it, let it spread forth, anoint this dish with ghee! As the lowing cow her young that craves the breast, ye gods shall greet with sounds of satisfaction this (porridge)!

38. With ghee thou hast covered it, hast made this place (for the porridge): may it, peerless, spread afar to heaven! Upon it shall rest the mighty eagle; gods shall offer it to the divinities!

39. Whatever the wife cooks aside from thee, (O husband), or the husband (cooks) unbeknown of thee, O wife, mix that together: to both of you it shall belong; bring it together into a single place!

40. As many of her children as dwell upon the earth, and the sons that have been begotten by him, all those ye shall call up to the dish: on shall come the young knowing their nest!

41. The goodly streams, swelling with honey, mixed with ghee, the seats of ambrosia, all these does he obtain, ascends to heaven. In sixty autumns the treasurer (of the porridge) shall fetch it!

42. The treasurer shall fetch this treasure: all outsiders round about shall not control it! The heaven-directed porridge, that has been presented and deposited by us, in three divisions has reached the thrte heavens.

43. May Agni burn the ungodly Rakshas; the flesh-devouring Pisâka shall have nothing here to partake of! We drive him away, hold him afar from us: the Âdityas and Angiras shall stay near it!

44. To the Âdityas and the Angiras do I offer this (food of) honey, mixed with ghee. Do ye two, (man and wife), with clean hands, without having injured a Brâhmana, performing pious deeds, go to that heavenly world!

45. I would obtain this highest part of it (the porridge), the place from which the highest lord permeates (the all). Pour butter upon it, anoint it witb plentiful ghee: this here is our share, fit for the Angiras!

46. For the sake of truth and holy strength do we make over this porridge as a hoarded treasure to the gods: it shall not be lost to us in gaming or in the assembly; do not let it go to any other person before me!

47. I cook, and I give (to the Brahmans), and so, too, my wife, at my religious rite and practice.--With the birth of a son the world of children has arisen (for you): do ye two hold on to a life that extends beyond (your years)!

48. In that place exists no guilt, and no duplicity, not even if he goes conspiring with his friends. This full dish of ours has here been deposited: the cooked (porridge) shall come back again to him that cooks it!

49. kind deeds we shall perform for our friends: all that hate us shall go to darkness (hell)!--As (fruitful) cow, and (strong) steer, they (man and wife) shall during, every successive period of their lives drive away man-besetting death!

50. The fires (all) know one another, that which lives in plants, and lives in the waters, and all the (light-) gods that glow upon the heaven. The gold (here) becomes the light of him that cooks (the porridge).

51. This (naked skin) among the hides is born upon man (alone), all other animals are riot naked. Clothe yourselves, (ye Brahmans), in sheltering garments: (even) the face of the porridge is a homespun garment!

52. What falsehood thou shalt speak at play and in the assembly, or the falsehood that thou shalt speak through lust for gain--put on together, (O man and wife), this same garment, deposit upon it every blemish!

53. Produce rain, go to the gods, let smoke arise from (thy) surface; all-embracing, about to be covered with ghee, enter as a co-dweller this place!

54. In many ways heaven assumes within itself a different form, according to circumstances. It (the heaven) has laid aside its black form, purifying itself to a bright (form); the red form do I sacrifice fot thee into the fire.

55. Thee here we hand over to the eastern direction, to Agni as sovereign lord, to the black serpent as guardian, to Âditya as bowman: do ye guard it for us, until we arrive! To the goal here he shall lead us, to old age; old age

shall hand us over to death: then shall we be united with the cooked (porridge)!

56. Thee here we hand over to the southern direction, to Indra as sovereign lord, to the serpent that is striped across as guardian, to Yama as bowman: do ye guard it for us, until we arrive! To the goal here, &c.

57. Thee here we hand over to the western direction, to Varuna as sovereign lord, to the pridâku-serpent as guardian, to food as bowman: do ye guard it for us, until we arrive. To the goal here, &c.

58. Thee here we hand over to the northern direction, to Soma as sovereign lord, to the svaga-serpent as guardian, to the lightning as bowman: do ye guard it for us, until we arrive. To the goal here, &c.

59. Thee here we hand over to the direction of the nadir, to Vishnu as sovereign lord, to the serpent with black-spotted neck as guardian, to the plants as bowmen: do ye guard it for us, until we arrive. To the goal here, &c.

60. Thee here we hand over to the direction of the zenith, to Brihaspati as sovereign lord, to the light-coloured serpent as guardian, to the rain as bowman: do ye guard it for us, until we arrive. To the goal here, &c.

IX, 3. Removal of a house that has been presented to a priest as sacrificial reward

1. The fastenings of the buttresses, the supports, and also of the connectinc, beams of the house, that abounds in treasures, do we loosen.

2. O (house) rich in all treasures! the fetter which has been bound about thee, and the knot which has been fastened upon thee, that with my charm do I undo, as Brihaspati (undid) Vala.

3. (The builder) has drawn thee to,,ether, pressed thee together, placed firm knots upon thee. Skilfully, as the priest who butchers (the sacrificial animal), do we with Indra's aid disjoint thy limbs.

4. From thy beams, thy bolts, thy frame, and thy thatch; from thy sides, (O house) abounding in treasures, do we loosen the fastenings.

5. The fastenings of the dove-tailed (joints), of the reed (-covering), of the frame-work, do we loosen here from the 'mistress of dwelling.'

6. The ropes which they have tied within thee for comfort, these do we loosen from thee; be thou propitious to our persons, O mistress of dwelling, after thou hast (again) been erected!

7. A receptacle for Soma, a house for Agni, a seat for the mistresses (of the house), a seat (for the priests), a seat for the gods art thou, O goddess house!

8. Thy covering of wicker-work, with thousand eyes, stretched out upon thy crown, fastened down and laid on, do we loosen with (this) charm.

9. He who receives thee as a gift, O house, and he by whom thou hast been built, both these, O mistress of dwelling, shall live attaining old age!

10. Return to him in the other world, firmly bound, ornamented, (thou house), which we loosen limb by limb, and joint by joint!

11. He who built thee, O house, brought together (thy) timbers, he, a Pragâpati on high, did construct thee, O house, for his progeny (pragâyai).

12. We render obeisance to him (the builder); obeisance to the giver, the lord of the house; obeisance to Agni who serves (the sacrifice); and obeisance to thy (attendant) man!

13. Reverence to the cattle and the horses, and to that which is born in the house! Thou that hast produced, art rich in offspring, thy fetters do we loosen.

14. Thou dost shelter Agni within, (and) the domestics together with the cattle. Thou that hast produced, art rich in offspring, thy fetters do we loosen.

15. The expanse which is between heaven and earth, with that do I receive as a gift this house of thine; the middle region which is stretched out from the sky, that do I make into a receptacle for treasures; with that do I receive the house for this one.

16. Full of nurture, full of milk, fixed upon the earth, erected, holding food for all, O house, do thou not injure them that receive thee as a gift!

17. Enveloped in grass, clothed in reeds, like night does the house lodge the cattle; erected thou dost stand upon the earth, like a she-elephant, firm of foot.

18. The part of thee that was covered with mats unfolding do I loosen. Thee that hast been enfolded by Varuna may Mitra uncover in the morning!

19. The house built with pious word, built by seers, erected--may Indra and Agni, the two immortals, protect the house, the seat of Soma!

20. Chest is crowded upon chest, basket upon basket; there mortal man is begotten from whom all things spring.

21. In the house which is built with two facades, four facades, six facades; in the house with eight facades, with ten facades, in the 'mistress of dwelling.' Agni rests as if in the womb.

Tuirning towards thee that art turned towards me, O house, I come to thee that injurest me not. For Agni and the waters, the first door to divine order, are within.

23. These waters, free from disease, destructive of disease, do I bring here. The chambers do I enter in upon in company with the immortal Agni (fire).

24. Do thou not fasten a fetter upon us; though a heavy load, become thou light! As a bride do we carry thee, O house, wherever we please.

25. From the easterly direction of the house reverence (be) to greatness, hail to the gods who are to be addressed with hail!

26. From the southerly direction of the house, &c.!
27. From the westerly direction of the house, &c.!
28. From the northerly direction of the house, &c.!
29. From the firm direction (nadir) of the house, &c.!
30. From the upright direction (zenith) of the house, &c.!

3 1. From every direction of the house reverence (be) to greatness, hail to the gods who are to be addressed with hail!

VI, 71. Brahmanical prayer at the receipt of gifts

1. The varied food which I consume in many places, my gold, my horses, and, too, my cows, goats, and sheep: everything whatsoever that I have received as a gift--may Agni, the priest, render that an auspicious offering!

2. The gift that has come to me by sacrifice, or without sacrifice, bestowed by the Fathers, granted by men, through which my heart, as it were, lights up with joy--may Agni, the priest, render that an auspicious offering!

3. The food that I, O gods, improperly consume, (the food) I promise, intending to give of it (to the Brahmans), or not to give of it, by the might of mighty Vaisvânara (Agni) may (that) food be for me auspicious and full of honey!

XX, 127. A kuntâpa-hymn

A

1. Listen, ye folks, to this: (a song) in praise of a hero shall be sung! Six thousand and ninety (cows) did we get (when we were) with Kaurama among the Rusamas,--

2. Whose twice ten buffaloes move right along, touether with their cows; the height of his chariot just misses the heaven which recedes from its touch.

3. This one (Kaurama) presented the seer with a hundred jewels, ten chaplets, three hundred steeds, and ten thousand cattle.

B

4. Disport thyself, O chanter, disport thyself as a bird upon a flowering tree; thy tongue glides quickly over the lips as a razor over the strop.

5. The chanters with their pious song hurry on blithely as cows; at home are their children, and at home the cows do they attend.

6. Bring hither, O chanter, thy poem, that which earns cattle and earns good things! Among the gods (kings) place thy voice as a manly archer his arrow!

C

7. Listen ye to the high praise of the king who rules over all peoples, the god who is above mortals, of Vaisvânara Parikshit!

8. 'Parikshit has procured for us a secure dwelling when he, the most excellent one, weat to his seat.' (Thus) the husband in Kuru-land, when he founds his household, converses with his wife.

9. 'What may I bring to thee, curds, stirred drink, or liquor?' (Thus) I the wife asks her husband in the kingdom of king Parikshit.

10. Like light the ripe barley runs over beyond the mouth (of the vessels). The people thrive merrily in the kingdom of king Parikshit.

D

11. Indra has awakened the poet, saying: 'Arise, move about, and sing; of me, the strong, verily, sing the praises; full every pious one shall offer thee (sacrificial reward)!'

12. Here, O cattle, ye shall be born, here, ye horses, here, ye domestics! And Pûshan also, who bestows a thousand (cows) as sacrificial reward, settles down here.

13. May these cattle, O Indra, not suffer harm, and may their owner not suffer harm; may the hostile folk, O Indra, may the thief not gain possession of them!

14. We shout to the hero with hymn and song we (shout) with a pleasing song. Take delight in our songs; may we not ever suffer harm!

COSMOGONIC AND THEOSOPHIC HYMNS

XII, 1. Hymn to goddess Earth

1. Truth, greatness, universal order (rita), strength. consecration, creative fervour (tapas), spiritual exaltation (brahma), the sacrifice, support the earth. May this earth, the mistress of that which was and shall be, prepare for us a broad domain!

2. The earth that has heights, and slopes, and great plains, that supports the plants of manifold virtue, free from the pressure that comes from the midst of men, she shall spread out for us, and fit. herself for us!

3. The earth upon which the sea, and the rivers and the waters, upon which food and the tribes of men have arisen, upon which this breathing, moving life exists, shall afford us precedence in drinking!

4. The earth whose are the four regions of space, upon which food and the tribes of men have arisen, which supports the manifold breathing, moving thinas, shall afford us cattle and other possessions also!

5. The earth upon which of old the first men unfolded themselves, upon which the gods overcame the Asuras, shall procure for us (all) kinds of cattle, horses, and fowls, good fortune, and glory!

6. The earth that supports all, furnishes wealth, the foundation, the golden-breasted resting-place of all living creatures, she that supports Agni Vaisvânara (the fire), and mates with Indra, the bull, shall furnish us with property!

7. The broad earth, which the sleepless gods ever attentively guard, shall milk for us precious honey, and, moreover, besprinkle us with glory!

8. That earth which formerly was water upon the ocean (of space), which the wise (seers) found out by their skilful devices; whose heart is in the

highest heaven, immortal, surrounded by truth, shall bestow upon us brilliancy and strength, (and place us) in supreme sovereignty!

9. That earth upon which the attendant waters jointly flow by day and night unceasingly, shall pour out milk for us in rich streams, and, moreover, besprinkle us with glory!

10. The earth which the Asvins have measured, upon which Vishnu has stepped out, which Indra, the lord of might, has made friendly to himself; she, the mother, shall pour forth milk for me, the son!

11. Thy snowy mountain heights, and thy forests, O earth, shall be kind to us! The brown, the black, the red, the multi-coloured, the firm earth, that is protected by Indra, I have settled upon, not suppressed, not slain, not wounded.

12. Into thy rniddle set us, O earth, and into thy navel, into the nourishing strength that has grown tip from thy body; purify thyself for us! The earth is the mother, and I the son of the earth; Paro-anya is the father; he, too, shall save us!

13. The earth upon which they (the priests) inclose the altar (vedi), upon which they, devoted to all (holy) works, unfold the sacrifice, upon which are set up, in front of the sacrifice, the sacrificial posts, erect and brilliant, that earth shall prosper us, herself prospering!

14. Him that hates us, O earth, him that battles against us, him that is hostile towards us with his mind and his weapons, do thou subject to us, anticipating (our wish) by deed!

15. The mortals born of thee live on thee, thou supportest both bipeds and quadrupeds. Thine, O earth, are these five races of men, the mortals, upon whom the rising sun sheds undying light with his rays.

16. These creatures all together shall yield milk for us; do thou, O earth, give us the honey of speech!

17. Upon the firm, broad earth, the all-begetting mother of the plants, that is supported by (divine) law, upon her, propitious and kind, may we ever pass-our lives!

18. A great gathering-place thou, great (earth), hast become; great haste, commotion, and agitation are upon thee. Great Indra protects thee unceasingly. Do thou, O earth, cause us to brighten as if at the sight of gold: not any one shall hate us!

19. Agni (fire) is in the earth, in the plants, the waters hold Agni, Agni is in the stones; Agni is within men, Agnis (fires) are within cattle, within horses.

20. Agni glows from the sky, to Agni, the god, belongs the broad air. The mortals kindle Agni, the bearer of oblations, that loveth ghee.

21. The earth, clothed in Agni, with dark knees, shall make me brilliant and alert!
22. Upon the earth men give to the gods the sacrifice, the prepared oblation; upon the earth mortal men live pleasantly by food. May this earth give us breath and life, may she cause me to reach old age!

23. The fragrance, O earth, that has arisen upon thee, which the plants and the waters hold, which the Gandharvas and the Apsaras have partaken of, with that make me fragrant: not any one shall hate us!

24. That fragrance of thine which has entered into the lotus, that fragrance, O earth, which the immortals of yore gathered up at the marriage of Sûryâ, with that make me fragrant: not any one shall hate us!

25. That fragrance of thine which is in men, the loveliness and charm that is in male and female, that which is in steeds and heroes, that which is in the wild animals with trunks (elephants), the lustre that is in the maiden, O earth, with that do thou blend us: not any one shall hate us!

26. Rock, stone, dust is this earth; this earth is supported, held together. To this golden-breasted earth I have rendered obeisance.

27. The earth, upon whom the forest-sprung trees ever stand firm, the all-nourishing, compact earth, do we invoke.

28. Rising or sitting, standing or walking, may we not stumble with our right or left foot upon the earth!

29. To the pure earth I speak, to the ground, the soil that has grown through the brahma (spiritual exaltation). Upon thee, that holdest nourishment, prosperity, food, and ghee, we would settle down, O earth!

30. Purified the waters shall flow for our bodies; what flows off from us that do we deposit upon him we dislike: with a purifier, O earth, do I purify myself!

31. Thy easterly regions, and thy northern, thy southerly (regions), O earth, and thy western, shall be kind to me as I walk (upon thee)! May I that have been placed into the world not fall down!

32. Do not drive us from the west, nor from the east; not from the north, and not from the south! Security be thou for us, O earth: waylayers shall not find us, hold far away (their) murderous weapon!

33. As long as I look out upon thee, O earth, with Sûrya (the sun) as my companion, so long shall my sight not fall, as year followeth upon year!

34. When, as I lie, I turn upon my right or left side, O earth; when stretched out we lie with our ribs upon thee pressing against (us), do not, O earth, that liest close to everything, there injure us!

35. What, O earth, I dig out of thee, quickly shall that grow again: may I not, O pure one, pierce thy vital spot, (and) not thy heart!

36. Thy summer, O earth, thy rainy season, thy autumn, winter, early spring, and spring; thy decreed yearly seasons, thy days and nights shall yield us milk

37. The pure earth that starts in fright away from the serpent, upon whom were the fires that are within the waters, she that delivers (to destruction) the blasphemous Dasyus, she that takes the side of Indra, not of Vritra, (that earth) adheres to Sakra (mighty Indra), the lusty bull.

38. Upon whom rests the sacrificial hut (sadas) and the (two) vehicles that hold the soma (havirdhâne), in whom the sacrificial post is fixed, upon whom the Brâhmanas praise (the gods) with riks and sâmans, knowing (also) the yagur-formulas; upon whom the serving-priests (ritvig) are employed so that Indra shall drink the soma;--

39. Upon whom the seers of yore, that created the beings, brought forth with their songs the cows, they the seven active (priests), by means of the satra-offerings, the sacrifices, and (their) creative fervour (tapas);--

40. May this earth point out to us the wealth that we-crave; may Bhaga (fortune) add his help, may Indra come here as (our) champion!

41. The earth upon whom the noisy mortals sing and dance, upon whom they fight, upon whom resounds the roaring drum, shall drive forth our enemies, shall make us free from rivals!

42. To the earth upon whom are food, and rice and barley, upon whom live these five races of men, to the earth, the wife of Parganya, that is fattened by rain, be reverence!

43. The earth upon whose ground the citadels constructed by the gods unfold themselves, every region of her that is the womb of all, Pragâpati shall make pleasant for us!

44. The earth that holds treasures manifold in secret places, wealth, jewels, and gold shall she give to me; she that bestows wealth liberally, the kindly goddess, wealth shall she bestow upon us!

45. The earth that holds people of manifold varied speech, of different customs, according to their habitations, as a reliable milch-cow that does not kick, shall she milk for me a thousand streams of wealth!

46. The serpent, the scorpion with thirsty fangs, that hibernating torpidly lies upon thee; the worm, and whatever living thing, O earth, moves in the rainy season, shall, when it creeps, not creep upon us: with what is auspicious (on thee) be gracious to us!

47. Thy many paths upon which people go, thy tracks for chariots and wagons to advance, upon which both good and evil men proceed, this road, free from enemies, and free from thieves, may we gain: with what is auspicious (on thee) be gracious to us!

48. The earth holds the fool and holds the wise, endures that good and bad dwell (upon her); she keeps company with the boar, gives herself up to the wild hog.

49. Thy forest animals, the wild animals homed in the woods, the man-eating lions, and tigers that roam; the ula, the wolf, mishap, injury (rikshikâ), and demons (rakshas), O earth, drive away from us!

50. The Gandharvas, the Apsaras, the Arâyas and Kimîdins; the Pisâkas and all demons (rakshas), these, O earth, hold from us!

51. The earth upon whom the biped birds fly together, the flamingoes, eagles, birds of prey, and fowls; upon whom Mâtarisvan, the wind, hastens, raising the dust, and tossing the trees-as the wind blows forth and back the flame bursts after;--

52. The earth upon whom day and night jointly, black and bright, have been decreed, the broad earth covered and enveloped with rain, shall kindly place us into every pleasant abode!

53. Heaven, and earth, and air have here given me expanse; Agni, Sûrya, the waters, and all the gods together have given me wisdom.

54. Mighty am I, 'Superior' (uttara) by name, upon the earth, conquering am I, all-conquering, completely conquering every region.

55. At that time, O goddess, when, spreading., (prathamânâ) forth, named (prithivî 'broad') by the gods, thou didst extend to greatness, then prosperity did enter thee, (and) thou didst fashion the four regions.

56. In the villages and in the wilderness, in the assembly-halls that are upon the earth; in the gatherings, and in the meetings, may we hold forth agreeably to thee!

57. As dust a steed did she, as soon as she was born, scatter these people, that dwelt upon the earth, she the lovely one, the leader, the guardian of the world, that holds the trees and plants.

58. The words I speak, honied do I speak them: the things I see they furnish me with. Brilliant I am and alert: the others that rush (against me) do I beat down.

59. Gentle, fragrant, kindly, with the sweet drink (kîlâla) in her udder, rich in milk, the broad earth together with (her) milk shall give us courage!

60. She whom Visvakarman (the creator of all) did search out by means of oblations, when she had entered the surging (flood of the) atmosphere, she, the vessel destined to nourish, deposited in a secret place, became visible (to the gods) and the (heavenly) mothers.

61. Thou art the scatterer of men, the broadly expanding Aditi that yields milk according to wish. What is wanting in thee Pragâpati, first-born of the divine order (rita), shall supply for thee

62. Thy laps, O earth, free from ailment! Free from disease, shall be produced for us! May we attentively, throuoh our long lives, be bearers of bali-offerings to thee!

63. O mother earth, kindly set me down upon a well-founded place! With (father) heaven cooperating, O thou wise one, do thou place me into happiness and prosperity!

XIII, 1. Prayer for sovereign power addressed to the god Rohita and his female Rohinî

1. Rise up, O steed, that art within the waters, enter this kingdom, rich in liberal gifts! Rohita (the red sun) who has begotten this all, shall keep thee well-supported for sovereignty!

2. The steed that is within the waters has risen up: ascend upon the clans that are sprung from thee! Furnishing soma, the waters, plants, and cows, cause thou four-footed and two-footed creatures to enter here!

3. Do ye, strong Maruts, children of Prisni (the cloud), allied with Indra, crush the enemies! Rohita shall hear you, that give abundant gifts, the thrice seven Maruts, who take delight in sweet (nourishment)!

4. Rohita has climbed the heights, he has ascended them, he, the embryo of women, (has ascended) the womb of births. Closely united with these women they found out the six broad (directions); spying out a road he has brought hither sovereignty.

5. Hither to thee Rohita has brought sovereignty; he has dispersed the enemies: freedom from danger has resulted for thee. To thee heaven and earth together with the revatî and sakvarî-stanzas shall yield gifts at will!

6. Rohita produced heaven and earth; there Parameshthin (the lord on high) extended the thread (of the sacrifice). There Aga Ekapâda (the one-footed goat, the sun) did fix himself; he made firm the heavens and earth with his strength.

7. Rohita made firm heaven and earth, by him the (heavenly) light was established, by him the firmament. By him the atmosphere and the spaces were measured out, through him the gods obtained immortality.

8. Rohita did ponder the multiform (universe) while preparing (his) climbings and advances. Having ascended the heaven with great might, he shall anoint thy royalty with milk and ghee!

9. All thy climbings, advances, and all thy ascents with which thou, (Rohita, the sun), fillest the heavens and the atmosphere, having strengthened thyself with their brahma and payas (spiritual and physical essence) do thou keep awake (do thou watch over) among the people in the kingdom of the (earthly) Rohita (the king)!

10. The peoples that have originated from thy tapas (heat, or creative fervour), have followed here the calf, the gâyatri. They shall enter thee with kindly spirit; the calf Rohita with its mother shall come on!

11. High on the firmament Rohita has stood, a youth, a sage, begettinu all forms. As Agni he shines with piercing light, in the third space he did assume lovely (forms).

12. A bull with a thousand horns, Gâtavedas (fire), endowed with sacrifices of ghee, carrying soma upon his back, rich in heroes, he shall, when implored, not abandon me, nor may I abandon thee: abundance in cattle and abundance in heroes procure for me!

14. Rohita is the generator of the sacrifice, and its mouth; to Rohita I offer oblations with voice, ear, and mind. To Rohita the gods resort with glad mind: he shall cause me to rise through elevation derived from the assembly!

14. Rohita arranged a sacrifice for Visvakarman; from it these brilliant, qualities have come to me. Let me announce thy origin over the extent of the world!

15, Upon thee have ascended the brihatî and the pankti (metres), upon thee the kakubh with splendour, O Gâtavedas. Upon thee the vashat-call, whose syllables make an ushnihâ, has ascended, upon thee Rohita with his seed has ascended.

16. This one clothes himself in the womb of the earth, this one clothes himself in heaven, and in the atmosphere. This one at the station of the brown (sun) did attain unto the worlds of light.

17. O Vâkaspati (lord of speech), the earth shall be pleasant to us, pleasant our dwelling, agrecable our couches! Right here life's breath shall be to our friend; thee, O Parameshthin, Agni shall envelop in life and lustre!

18. O Vâkaspati, the five seasons that we have, which have come about as the creation of Visvakarman, rialit here (they and) life's breath shall be to our friend; thee, O Parameshthin, Rohita shall envelop in life and lustre!

19. O Vâkaspati, good cheer and spirit, cattle in our stable, children in our wombs beget thou! Right here life's breath shall be to our friend; thee, O Parameshthin, I envelop in life and lustre.

20. God Savitar and Agni shall envelop thee, Mitra and Varuna surround thee with lustre! Treading down all powers of grudge come thou hither: thou hast made this kingdom rich in liberal gifts.

21. Thou, O Rohita, whom the brindled cow, harnessed at the side, carries, goest with brilliance, causing the waters to flow.

22. Devoted to Rohita is Rohinî his mistress, with beautiful colour (complexion), great, and lustrous: through her may we conquer booty of every description, through her win every battle!

23. This seat, Rohinî, belongs to Rohita; yonder is the path on which the brindled (female) goes! Her the Gandharvas and the Kasyapas lead forth, her the sages guard with diligence.

24. The radiant bay steeds of the sun, the immortal, ever draw the delightful chariot. Rohita, the drinker of ghee, the shining god, did enter the variegated heavens.

25. Rohita, the sharp-horned bull, who surpasses Agni and surpasses Sûrya, who props up the earth and the sky, out of him the gods frame the creations.

26. Rohita ascended the heaven from the great flood; Rohita has climbed all heights.
27. Create (the cow) that is rich in milk, drips with ghee: she is the milch-cowof the gods that does not refuse! Indra shall drink the Soma, there shall be secure possession; Agni shall sing praises: the enemies do thou drive out!

28. Agni kindled, spreads his flames, fortified by ghee, sprinkled with ghee. Victorious, all-conquering Agni shall slay them that are my rivals!

29. He shall slay them, shall burn the enemy that battles against us! With the flesh-devouring Agni do we burn our rivals.

30. Smite them down, O Indra, with the thunderbolt, with thy (strong) arm! Then have I overpowered my rivals with Agni's brilliant strengths.

31. O Agni, subject our rivals to us; confuse, O Brihaspati, the kinsman that is puffed up! O Indra and Agni, O Mitra and Varuna, subjected they shall be, unable to vent their wrath against us!

32. Do thou, god Sûrya (the sun), when thou risest, beat down my rivals, beat them down with a stone: they shall go to the nethermost darkness!

33. The calf of Virâg, the bull of prayers, carrying the bright (soma) upon his back, has ascended the atmosphere. A song accompanied by ghee they sing to the calf; himself brahma (spiritual exaltation) they swell him with their brahma (prayer).

34. Ascend the heavens, ascend the earth sovereignty ascend thou, and possessions ascend thou! Offspring ascend thou, and immortality ascend thou, unite thy body with Rohita!

35. The gods that hold sovereignty, who go about the sun, with these allied, Rohita, kindly disposed, shall bestow sovereignty upon thee!

36. The sacrifices purified by prayer lead thee forth; the bay steeds that travel upon the road carry thee: thou shinest across the swelling ocean.

37. In Rohita who conquers wealth, conquers cattle, and conquers booty, heaven and earth are fixed. Of thee that hast a thousand and seven births, let me announce the origin over the extent of the world!

38. Glorious thou goest to the intermediate directions and the directions (of space), glorious (in the sight) of animals and the tribes of men, glorious in the lap of the earth, of Aditi: may I like Savitar be lovely!

39. Being yonder thou knowest (what takes place) here; being here thou beholdest these things. Here (men) behold the inspired sun that shines upon the sky.

40. A god thou praisest the gods, thou movest within the flood. They kindle (him), a universal fire; him the highest sages know.

41. Below the superior (region), above the inferior (region) here, the cow has arisen supporting (her) calf by the foot. Whither is she turned; to which half (of the universe), forsooth, has she aone away; where, forsooth, does she beget? Verily not in this herd!

42. One-footed, two-footed, four-footed is she; eight-footed, nine-footed became she, the thousand-syllabled (consisting of thousand elements) pankti (quinary stanza) of the universe: the oceans from her flow forth upon (the world).

43. Ascending the heaven, immortal, receive kindly my song! The sacrifices purified by prayer lead thee forth; the bay steeds that travel upon the road carry thee.

44. That do I know of thee, O immortal, where thy march is upon the sky, where thy habitation is in the highest heaven.

45. Sûrya (the sun) surveys the sky, Sûrya the earth, Sûrya the waters. Sûrya is the single eye of being: he has ascended the great heavens.

46. The broad (directions) where the fagots that fence in (the fire), the earth turned itself into a fire-altar. There Rohita laid on for himself these two fires, cold and heat.

47. Laying on cold and heat, using the mountains as sacrificial posts, the two fires of Rohita who knows the (heavenly) light, into which (the fires) rain (flowed) as ghee, carried out the sacrifice.

48. The fire of Rohita who knows the (heavenly) light is kindled by prayer. From it heat, from it cold, from it the sacrifice was produced.

49. The two fires swelling through prayer, increased through prayer, sacrificed into with prayer; the two fires of Rohita who knows the (heavenly) light, kindled through prayer, carried out the sacrifice.

50. One is deposited in truth, the other is kindled in the waters. The two fires of Rohita who knows the (heavenly) light, kindled through prayer, carried out the sacrifice.

51. The fire which the wind brightens up, and that which Indra and Brahmanaspati (brighten up), the two fires of Rohita who knows the (heavenly) light, kindled through prayer, carried out the sacrifice.

52. Having fashioned the earth into an altar, having made the heavens (his) sacrificial reward, then having made heat into fire, Rohita created all that has breath through rain (serving) as ghee.

53. Rain fashioned itself into ghee, heat into fire, the earth into an altar. Then Agni by (his) songs fashioned the high mountains.

54. Having fashioned by means of songs the high (mountains), Rohita spake to the earth: In thee all shall be born, what is and what shall be.

55. The sacrifice first, (and then) what is and what shall be was born. From that this all was born, and whatever here appears, brought hither by the sage Rohita.

56. He who kicks a cow with his foot, and he who micturates towards the sun--of thee do I tear out the root; thou shalt henceforth not cast a shadow!

57. Thou that passest across me, casting thy shadow against me, between me and the fire--of thee do I tear out the root; thou shalt henceforth not cast a shadow!

58. He, O god Sûrya, that to-day passes between thee and me, upon him our evil dream, our foulness, and our misfortunes do we wipe off.

59. May we not miss our way, may we not, O Indra, miss the sacrifice of him that presses the soma; may.not the powers of grudge intercept us!

60. The (guiding) thread stretched out among the gods, that accomplishes the sacrifice, that, by pouring oblations, may we attain!

XI, 5. Glorification of the sun, or the primeval principle, as a Brahman disciple

1. The Brahmakârin (Brahmanical disciple) moves inciting both hemispheres of the world; in him the gods are harmonised. He holds the heavens and the earth, he fills the teacher with creative fervour (tapas).

2. The fathers, the divine folk, and all the gods severally follow the Brahmakârin; the Gandharvas did go after him, six thousand three hundred and thirty-three. He fills all the gods with creative fervour.

3. When the teacher receives the Brahmakârin as a disciple, he places him as a foetus inside (of his body). He carries him for three nights in his belly: when he is born the gods gather about to see him.

4. This earth is (his first) piece of firewood, the heaven the second, and the atmosphere also he fills with (the third) piece of firewood. The Brahmakârin. fills the worlds with his firewood, his girdle, his asceticism, and his creative fervour.

5. Prior to the brahma (spiritual exaltation) the Brahmakârin was born; clothed in heat, by creative fervour he arose. From him sprung the brâhmanam (Brahmanic life) and the highest brahma, and all the gods together with immortality (amrita).

6. The Brahmakârin advances, kindled by the firewood, clothed in the skin of the black antelope, consecrated, with long beard. Within the day he passes from the eastern to the northern sea; gathering together the worlds he repeatedly shapes them.

7. The Brahmakârin, begetting the brahma, the waters, the world, Pragâpati Parameshthin (he that stands in the hiahest place), and Virâg, having become an embryo in the womb of immortality, having forsooth, become Indra, pierced the Asuras.

8. The teacher fashioned these two hern spheres of the world, the broad and the deep, earth and heaven. These the Brahmakârin guards with his creative fervour (tapas): in him the gods are harmonised.

9. This broad earth and the heaven the Brahmakârin first brought hither as alms. Having made these into two sticks of firewood he reveres them upon them all beings have been founded.

10. One is on the hither side, the other on the farther side of the back of the heavens; secretly are deposited the two receptacles of the brâhmanam (Brahmanic life). These the Brahmakârin protects by his tapas (creative fervour); understandingly he performs that brahma (spiritual exaltation) solely.

11. One on the hither side, the other away from the earth, do the two Agnis come together between these two hemispheres (of the world). To them adhere the rays firmly; the Brahmakârin by his tapas (creative fervour) enters into the (rays).

12. Shouting forth, thundering, red, white he carries a great penis along the earth. The Brahmakârin sprinkles seed upon the back of the earth; through it the four directions live.

13. Into fire, the sun, the moon, Mâtarisvan (wind), and the waters, the Brahmakârin places the firewood; the lights from these severally go into the clouds, from them come sacrificial butter, the purusha (primeval man), rain, and water.

14. Death is the teacher, (and) Varuna, Soma, the plants, milk; the clouds were the warriors: by these this light has been brought hither.

15. Varuna, having become the teacher, at home prepares the ghee solely. Whatever he desired from Pragâpati, that the Brahmakârin furnished, as Mitra (a friend) from his own Atman (spirit, or person).

16. The Brahmakârin is the teacher, the Brahmakârin Pragâpati. Pragâpati rules (shines forth, vi râgati); Virâg (heavenly power, or light) became Indra, the ruler.

17. Through holy disciplehood. (brahmakâryam), through tapas (creative fervour), the king protects his kingdom. The teacher by (his own) brahmakâryam (holy life) seeks (finds) the Brahmakârin.

18. Through holy disciplehood the maiden obtains a young husband, through holy disciplehood the steer, the horse seeks to obtain fodder.

19. Through holy disciplehood, through creative fervour, the gods drove away death. Indrajorsooth, by his holy disciplehood brought the light to the gods.

20. The plants, that which was and shall be, day and night, the tree, the year along with the seasons, have sprung from the Brahmakârin.

21. The earthly and the heavenly animals, the wild and the domestic, the wingless and the winged (animals), have sprung from the Brahmakârin.

22. All the creatures of Pragâpati (the creator) severally carry breath in their souls. All these the brahma, which has been brought hither in the Brahmakârin, protects.

23. This, that was set into motion by the gods, that is insurmountable, that moves shining, from it has sprung the brâhmanam (Brahmanical life), the highest brahma, and all the gods, together with immortality (amrita).

24, 25. The Brahmakârin carries the shining brahma: into this all the gods are woven. Producing in-breathing and out-breathing, as well as through-breathing; speech, mind, heart, brahma, and wisdom, do thou furnish us with sight, hearing, glory, food, semen, blood, and belly!

26. These things the Brahmakârin fashioned upon the back of the (heavenly) water. He stood in the sea kindled with tapas (creative fervour). He, when he has bathed, shines vigorously upon the earth, brown and ruddy.

XI, 4. Prâna, life or breath, personified as the supreme spirit

1. Reverence to Prâna, to whom all this (universe) is subject, who has become the lord of the all, on whom the all is supported!

2. Reverence, O Prâna, to thy roaring (wind), reverence, O Prâna, to thy thunder, reverence, O Prâna, to thy lightning, reverence, O Prâna, to thy rain!

When Prâna calls aloud to the plants with his thunder, they are fecundated, they conceive, and then are produced abundant (plants).

4. When the season has arrived, and Prâna calls aloud to the plants, then everything rejoices, whatsoever is upon the earth.

5. When Prâna has watered the great earth with rain, then the beasts rejoice; (they think): 'strength, forsooth, we shall now obtain.'

6. When they had been watered by Prâna, the plants spake in concert: 'thou hast, forsooth, prolonged our life, thou hast made us all fragrant.'

7. Reverence be, O Prâna, to thee coming, reverence to thee going; 'reverence to thee standing, and reverence, too, to thee sitting!

8. Reverence be to thee, O Prâna, when thou breathest in (primate), reverence when thou breathest out! Reverence be to thee when thou art

turned away, reverence to thee when thou art turned hither: to thee, entire, reverence be here!

9. Of thy dear form, O Prâna, of thy very dear form, of the healing power that is thine, give unto us, that we may live!

10. Prâna clothes the creatures, as a father his dear son. Prâna, truly, is the lord of all, of all that breathes, and does not breathe.

11. Prâna is death, Prâna is fever. The gods worship Prana. Prâna shall place the truth-speaker in the highest world

12. Prâna is Virâg (power, lustre), Prâna is Deshtrî (the divinity that guides): all worship Prâna. Prâna verily is sun and moon. They call Prâna Pragâpati.

13. Rice and barley are in-breathing and outbreathing. Prâna is called a steer. In-breathing forsooth, is founded upon barley; rice is called out-breathing.

14. Man breathes out and breathes in when within the womb. When thou, O Prâna, quickenest him, then is he born again.

15. They call Prâna Mâtarisvan (the wind); Prâna, forsooth, is called Vâta (the wind). The past and the future, the all, verily is supported upon Prâna.

16. The holy (âtharvana) plants, the magic (ângirasa) plants, the divine plants, and those produced by men, spring forth, when thou, O Prâna, quickenest them.

17, When Prâna has watered the great earth with rain, then the plants spring forth, and also every sort of herb.

18. Whoever, O Prâna, knows this regarding thee, and (knows) on what thou art supported, to him all shall offer tribute in yonder highest world.

19. As all these creatures, O Prâna, offer thee tribute, so they shall offer tribute (in yonder world) to him who hears thee, O far-famed one!

20. He moves as an embryo within the gods; having arrived, and being in existence, he is born again. Having arisen he enters with his mights the present and the future, as a father (goes to) his son.

21. When as a swan he rises from the water he does not withdraw his one foot. If in truth he were to withdraw it, there would be neither to-day, nor to-morrow, no night and no day, never would the dawn appear.

22. With eight wheels, and one felloe he moves, containing a thousand sounds (elements), upward in the east, downward in the west. With (his) half he produced the whole world: what is the visible sign of his (other) half?

23. He who rules over this (all) derived from every source, and over everything that movesreverence be to thee, O Prâna, that wieldest a swift bow against others (the enemies)!

24. May Prâna, who rules over this (all) derived from every source, and over everything that moves, (may he) unwearied, strong through the brahma, adhere to me!

25. Erect he watches in those that sleep, nor does lie lie down across. No one has heard of his sleeping in those that sleep.

26. O Prâna, be not turned away from me, thou shalt not be other than myself! As the embryo of the waters (fire), thee, O Prâna, do bind to me, that I may live.

IX, 2. Prayer to Kâma (love), personified as a primordial power

1. To the bull that slays the enemy, to Kâma, do I render tribute with ghee, oblation, and (sacrificial) melted butter. Do thou, since thou hast been extolled, hurl down my enemies by thy great might!

2. The evil dream which is offensive to my mind and eye, which harasses and does not please me, that (dream) do I let loose upon my enemy. Having praised Kâma may I prevail!

3,. Evil dreams, O Kâma, and misfortune, O Kâma, childlessness, ill-health, and trouble, do thou, a strong lord, let loose upon him that designs evil against us!

4. Drive them away, O Kâma, thrust them away, O Kâma; may they that are my enemies fall into trouble! When they have been driven into the nethermost darkness, do thou, O Agni, burn up their d welling- places!

5. That milch-cow, O Kâma, whom the sages call Vâk Virâg (ruling, or resplendent speech), is said to be thy daughter; by her drive away my enemies; breath, cattle, and life shall give them a wide birth!

6. With the strength of Kâma, Indra, king Varuna, and Vishnu, with the impelling force (savena) of Savitar, with the priestly power of Agni, do I drive forth the enemies, as a skilled steersman a boat.

7. My sturdy guardian, strong Kâma, shall procure for me full freedom from enmity! May the gods collectively be my refuge, may all the gods respond to this, my invocation!

8. Taking pleasure in this (sacrificial) melted butter, and ghee do ye, (O gods), of whom Kâma is the highest, be joyful in this place, procuring for me full freedom from enmity!

9. O Indra and Agni, and Kâma, having formed an alliance, do ye hurl down my enemies; when they have fallen into the nethermost darkness, do thou, O Agni, burn up after them their dwelling places!

10. Slay thou, O Kâma, those that are my enemies, hurl them down into blind darkness. Devoid of vigour, Without sap let them all be; they shall not live a single day!

11. Kâma has slain those that are my enemies, a broad space has he furnished me to thrive in. May the four directions of space bow down to me, and the six broad (regions) carry ghee to me!

12. They (the enemies) shall float down like a boat cut loose from its moorings! There is no returning again for those who have been struck by our missiles.

13. Agni is a defence, Indra a defence, Soma a defence. May the gods, who by their defence ward off (the enemy), ward him off!

14. With his men reduced, driven out, the hated (enemy) shall go, shunned by his own friends! And down upon the earth do the lightnings alight; may the strong god crush your enemies!

15. This mighty lightning supports both moveable and immoveable things, as well as all thunders. May the rising sun by his resources and his majesty hurl down my enemies, lie the mighty one!

16. With that triple-armoured powerful covering of thine, O Kâma, with the charm that has been made into an Invulnerate armour spread (over thee), with that do thou drive away those who are my enemies; may breath, cattle, and life give them a wide berth!

17. With the weapon with which the god drove forth the Asuras, with which Indra led the Dasyus to the nethermost darkness, with that do thou, O Kâma, drive forth far away from this world those who are my enemies!

18. As the gods drove forth the Asuras, as Indra. forced the demons into the nethermost darkness, thus do thou, O Kâma, drive forth far away from this world those who are my enemies!

19. Kâma was born at first; him neither the gods, nor the Fathers, nor men have equalled. To these art thou superior, and ever great; to thee, O Kâma, do I verily offer reverence.

20. As great as are the heavens and earth in extent, as far as the waters have swept, as far as fire; to these art thou superior, &c.

21. Great as are the directions (of space) and the intermediate direction on either side, great as are the regions and the vistas of the sky; to these art thou superior, &c.

22. As many bees, bats, kurûru-worms, as many vaghas and tree-serpents as there are; to these art thou superior, &c.

23. Superior art thou to all that winks (lives), superior to all that stands still (is not alive), superior to the ocean art thou, O Kâma, Manyu! To these art thou superior, &c.

24. Not, surely, does the wind equal Kâma, not the fire, not the sun, and not the moon. To these art thou superior, &c.

25. With those auspicious and gracious forms of thine, O Kâma, through which what thou wilst becometh reaL with these do thou enter into us, and elsewhere send the evil thoughts!

XIX, 53. Prayer to Kâla (time), personified as a primordial power

1. Time, the steed, runs with seven reins (rays), thousand-eyed, ageless, rich in seed. The seers, thinking holy thoughts, mount him, all the beings (worlds) are his wheels.

2. With seven wheels does this Time ride, seven naves has he, immortality is his axle. He carries hither all these beings (worlds). Time, the first god, now hastens onward.

3. A full jar has been placed upon Time; him, verily, we see existing in many forms. He carries away all these beings (worlds); they call him Time in the highest heaven.

4. He surely did bring hither all the beings (worlds), he surely did encompass all the beings (worlds). Being their father, he became their son; there is, verily, no other force, higher than he.

5. Time begot yonder heaven, Time also (begot) these earths. That which was, and that which shall be, urged forth by Time, spreads out.

6. Time created the earth, in Time the sun burns. In Time are all beings, in Time the eye looks abroad.
7. In Time mind is fixed, in Time breath (is fixed), in Time names (are fixed); when Time has arrived all these creatures rejoice.

8. In Time tapas (creative fervour) is fixed; in Time the highest (being is fixed); in Time brahma (spiritual exaltation) is fixed; Time is the lord of everything, he was the father of Pragâpati.

9. By him this (universe) was urged forth, by him it was begotten, and upon him this (universe) was founded. Time, truly, having become the brahma (spiritual exaltation), supports Parameshthin (the highest lord).

10. Time created the creatures (pragâh), and Time in the beginning (created) the lord of creatures (Prâgapati); the self-existing Kasyapa and the tapas (creative fervour) from Time were born.

XIX, 54. Prayer to Kâla (time), personified as a primordial power

1. From Time the waters did arise, from Time the brahma (spiritual exaltation), the tapas (creative fervour), the regions (of space did arise). Through Time the sun rises, in Time he goes down again.

2. Through Time the wind blows, through Time (exists) the great earth; the great sky is fixed in Time. In Time the son (Pragâpati) begot of yore that which was, and that which shall be.

3. From Time the Riks arose, the Yagus was born from Time; Time put forth the sacrifice, the imperishable share of the gods.

4. Upon Time the Gandharvas and Apsarases are founded, upon Time the worlds (are founded), in Time this Angiras and Atharvan rule over the heavens.

5. Having conquered this world and the highest world, and the holy (pure) worlds (and) their holy divisions; having by means of the brahma (spiritual exaltation) conquered all the worlds, Time, the highest God, forsooth, hastens onward.

XI, 7. Apotheosis of the ukkhishta, the leavings of the sacrifice

1. In the ukkhishta are deposited name (quality) and form, in the ukkhishta the world is deposited. Within the ukkhishta Indra and Agni, and the all are deposited.

2. In the ukkhishta heaven and earth, and all beings, are deposited; in the ukkhishta are deposited the waters, the ocean, the moon, and the wind.

3. In the ukkhishta are both being and non-being, death, strength (food), and Pragâpati. The (creatures) of the world are founded upon the ukkhishta; (also) that which is confined and that which is free, and the grace in me.

4. He who fastens what is firm, the strong, the leader, the brahma, the ten creators of the all, the divinities, are fixed on all sides to the ukkhishta as the (spokes of the) wheel to the nave.

5. Rik, Sâman, and Yagus, the singing of the sâmans, their introductions, and the stotras are in the ukkhishta. The sound 'him' is in the ukkhishta, and the modulations and the music of the sâman. That is in me.

6. The prayer to Indra and Agni (aindrâgnam), the call to the soma, as it is being purified (pâvamâmam), the mahânâmnî-verses, the singing of the mahâvrata, (these) divisions of the service are in the ukkhishta, as the embryo in the mother.

7. The ceremony of the consecration of the king (râgasûya), the vâgapeya, the agnishtoma, and the cattle-sacrifice belonging to it, the arka and the horse-sacrifice, and the most delightful (sacrifice) for which fresh barhis is strewn, are in the ukkhishta.

8. The preparation of the sacred fire (agnyâdheyam), the consecration for the soma-sacrifice (dikshâ), the sacrifice by which (special) wishes are fulfilled, together with the metres, the sacrifices that have passed out, and the extended sacrifices (satra), are lounded upon the ukkhishta.

9. The agnihotra, faith, the call vashat, vows and asceticism, sacrificial rewards, what is sacrificed (to the gods) and given (to the priests) are contained in the ukkhishta.

10. The (soma-sacrifice) that lasts one night (ekarâtra), and that which lasts two nights (dvirâtra), the (condensed soma-sacrifice called) sadyahkrî, and

(that which is called) prakrî, the (Songs called) ukthya, are woven and deposited in the ukkhishta; (also the parts) of the sacrifice subtle through (higher) knowledge.

11. The soma-sacrifice that lasts four nights (katûrâtra), five nights (pañkarâtra), six nights (shadrâtra), and along (with them) those that last double the time; the sixteenfold stotra (shodasin), and the soma-sacrifice that lasts seven nights (saptarâtra), all the sacrifices which were founded upon immortality (amrita), were begotten of the ukkhishta.

12. The pratihâra-passages (in the sâman-songs), and their final syllables, the (soma-sacrifices called) visvagit and abhgit, the soma-sacrifice that ends

with the day (sâhna), and that which lasts into the next day (atirâtra), are in the ukkhishta--the soma-sacrifice also that lasts twelve days. That is in me.

13. Liberality, accomplishment, possession, the call svadhâ, nurture, immortality (amrita), and might, all inner desires are satisfied according to wish in the ukkhishta.

14. The nine earths, oceans, heavens, are founded upon the ukkhishta. The sun shines in the ukkhishta, and day and night also. That is in me.

15. The (soma-sacrifice called) upahavya, the offering on the middle day of a sacrifice lasting a year (vishûvant), and the sacrifices that are secretly presented, Ukkhishta, the sustainer of the universe, the father of the generator (Pragâpati), supports.

16. Ukkhishta, the father of the generator, the grandson of the spirit (asu), the primal ancestor (grandfather), the ruler of the universe, the lusty bull dwells upon the earth.

17. Order (rita), truth (satya), creative fervour (tapas), sovereignty, asceticism, law and works; past, future, strength, and prosperity, are in the ukkhishta-force in force.

18. Success, might, plans, dominion, sovereignty, the six broad (regions), the year, libation (idâ), the orders to the priests (praisha), the draughts of soma (graha), oblations (are founded) upon the ukkhishta.

19. The (liturgies called) katurhotârah, the âpri-hymns, the triennial sacrifices, the (formulas called) nîvid, the sacrifices, the priestly functions,

the cattle-sacrifice and the soma-oblations connected with it, are in the ukkhishta.

20. The half-months and months, the divisions of the year together with the seasons, the resounding waters, thunder, the great Vedic canon (sruti) are in the ukkhishta.

21. Pebbles, sand, stones, herbs, plants, grass, clouds, lightning, rain, are attached to, and are founded upon the ukkhishta.

22. Success, attainment, accomplishment, control, greatness, prosperity, supreme attainment, and wellbeing rest upon, rest in, have been deposited in the ukkhishta.

23. Whatever breathes with breath, and sees with sight, all gods in the heavens, founded upon heaven, were born of the ukkhishta.

24. The riks and the sâmans, the metres, the ancient legends (purânam) together with the yagus, all gods in the heavens, founded upon heaven, were born of the ukkhishta.

25. In-breathing and out-breathing, sight, hearing, imperishableness and perishableness, all gods in the heavens, founded upon heaven, were born of the ukkhishta.

26. Joys, pleasures, delights, jubilation and merriment, all gods in the heavens, founded upon heaven, were born of the ukkhishta.

27. The gods, the (deceased) Fathers, men, Gandharvas and Apsaras, all gods in the heavens, founded upon heaven, were born of the ukkhishta.

IX, 1. Hymn to the honey-lash of the Asvins

1. From heaven, from earth, from the atmosphere, from the sea, from the fire, and from the wind, the honey-lash hath verily sprung. This, clothed in amrita (ambrosia), all the creatures revering, acclaim in their hearts.

2. Great sap of all forms (colours) it hath-they call thee moreover the seed of the ocean. Where the honey-lash comes bestowing gifts, there life's breath, and there immortality has settled down.

3. Men severally, contemplating it profoundly, behold its action upon the earth: from the fire and from the wind the honey-lash hath verily sprung, the strong child of the Maruts.

4. Mother of the Âdityas, daughter of the Vasus, breath of life of created beings, nave of immortality, the honey-lash, golden-coloured, dripping ghee, as a great embryo, moves among mortals.

5. The god's begot the lash of honey, from it came an embryo having all forms (colours). This, as soon as born, (while yet) young its mother nourishes; this, as soon as born, surveys all the worlds.

6. Who knows it and who perceives it, the inexhaustible, soma-holding cup that has come from the heart of it (the honey-lash)? 'Tis the wise priest: he shall derive inspiration from it!

7. He knows them, and he perceives them, the inexhaustible breasts of it (the honey-lash), that yield a thousand streams. Nourishment they pour out -without recalcitration.

8. The great (cow) that loudly gives forth the sound 'him,' that bestows strength, and goes with loud shouts to the holy act, bellowing with lust for the three (male) gharmas (fires), she lows, and drips with (streams) of milk.

9. When the waters, the mighty bulls, self-sovereign, wait upon (the cow), swollen with milk, (then) they, the waters, pour nourishment (upon her), and cause her to pour nourishment at will for him that knoweth this.

10. The thunder is thy voice, O Pragâpati; as a bull thou hurlest thy fire upon the earth. From the fire, and from the wind the honey-lash hath verily sprung, the strong child of the Maruts.

11. As the soma at the morn ing-pressure is dear to the Asvins, thus in my own person, O Asvins, lustre shall be sustained!

12. As the soma at the second (mid-day) pressure is dear to Indra and Agni, thus in my own person, O Indra, and Agni, lustre shall be sustained!

13. As the soma at the third pressure (evening) is dear to the Ribhus, thus in my own person, O Ribhus, lustre shall be sustained!

14. May I beget honey for myself; may I obtain honey for myself! Bringing milk, O Agni, I have come:. endow me with lustre!

15. Endow me, O Agni, with lustre, endow me with offspring and with life! May the gods take note of this (prayer) of mine; may Indra together with the Rishis (take note of it)!

16. As bees carry together honey upon honey, thus in my own person, O Asvins, lustre shall be sustained!

17. As the bees pile this honey upon honey, thus in my own person, O Asvins, lustre, brilliance, strength, and force shall be sustained!

18. The honey that is in the mountains, in the heights; in the cows, and in the horses; the honey which is in the surâ (brandy) as it is being poured out, that shall be in me!

19. O Asvins, lords of brightness, anoint me with the honey of the bee, that I may speak forceful speech among men!

20. The thunder is thy speech, O Pragâpati; as a bull thou hurlest thy fire upon earth and heaven. All animals live upon it (the earth), and she with it (Pragâpati's fire) fills nourishment and food.

21. The earth is the staff, the atmosphere the embryo, the heaven the whip (itself?), the lightning the whip-cord; of gold is the tip (of the whip?).

22. He that knoweth the seven honies of the whip becomes rich in honey; (to wit), the Brâhmana, the king, the cow, the ox, rice, barley, and honey as the seventh.

23. Rich in honey becomes he, rich in honey become his appurtenances, worlds rich in honey does he win, he that knoweth thus.

24. When in a bright sky it thunders, then Pragâpati manifests himself to (his) creatures (pragâh). Therefore do I stand with the sacred cord suspended from the right shoulder (prâkinopavita), saying, 'O Pragâpati,

watch over me!' The creatures (pragâh) watch over him, Pragâpati watches over him, that knoweth thus.

Read these similar books for free at forgottenbooks.org:

Clarence Darrow on Religion

The Texts of the White Yajurveda

The Devi Bhagavatam

The Transmigration of the Seven Brahmans

The Satapatha Brahmana

The Mahabharata

Hymns of the Samaveda

A Vedic Reader for Students

The Upanishads

The Vishnu Purana

Read or order online at:

www.forgottenbooks.org
or
www.amazon.com

987061

Printed in Great Britain by
Amazon.co.uk, Ltd.,
Marston Gate.